A
PIECE
OF THE
ACTION

A PIECE OF THE ACTION

How Women and Minorities Can Launch Their Own Successful Businesses

SUZANNE CAPLAN

amacom

American Management Association

New York • Atlanta • Boston • Chicago • Kansas City • San Francisco • Washington, D.C.
Brussels • Mexico City • Tokyo • Toronto

This publication is designed to provide accurate and authoritative information in regard to the subject matter covered. It is sold with the understanding that the publisher is not engaged in rendering legal, accounting, or other professional service. If legal advice or other expert assistance is required, the services of a competent professional person should be sought.

Library of Congress Cataloging-in-Publication Data

Caplan, Suzanne.
    A piece of the action : how women and minorities can launch their own successful businesses / Suzanne Caplan.
      p. cm.
    Includes bibliographical references and index.
    ISBN 0-8144-7896-7
    1. New business enterprises.   2. Small business—Management.
3. Women-owned business enterprises.   4. Minority business enterprises. I. Title.
    HD62.5.C366   1994
    658.1'141—dc20   93-42510
                                            CIP

Printing number

10 9 8 7 6 5 4 3 2 1

To
My
Niece
Harriet Schwartz
Who Understands and Believes
in Diversity

Contents

Preface

I have spent the last twenty-one years of my life as an entrepreneur. It hasn't always been easy, but it has always been interesting and challenging. The work can be hard and the hours extremely long. I still haven't learned all I need to know. And I love every minute—even the tough ones.

These are difficult economic times. Jobs are scarce and profits hard to find. But there are always opportunities for hardworking, creative people to build successful new businesses. If you are a woman or a member of a minority, you will have additional hurdles to jump. This book is intended to show you where they are and give you strategies to get around them. Knowledge is power.

Economic freedom is the ultimate equalizer, and it should be a goal of our society. Providing capital, training, and technical assistance for new business owners is a good first step to that end.

There are many government agencies, nonprofits, and business organizations committed to the new entrepreneurs. Find them and take advantage of what they offer. Your success is in everyone's best interest.

S.C.

Acknowledgments

A book is always a collaborative effort, and this one is no exception. As always, I am grateful to Sherry Truesdell, a woman entrepreneur, who turns my scribble into words, keeps it organized, and offers a valued opinion. Creating a project with my agent, Laurie Harper, is energizing, life-affirming, and just plain fun.

My AMACOM editor, Andrea Pedolsky, an uncompromising advocate for her readers and their needs, helped make my work customer-driven. It is the ultimate business insight.

To Tom Nunnally, the best small-business banker of all times: After almost twenty years, I continue to learn from you. And to some of the good folks at East Liberty Development, Inc.—Board Chair John Brown, Jr., Executive Director Karen LaFrance, and John Betzler: It is efforts such as yours that offer the greatest possibilities for aspiring entrepreneurs. I hope they learn that from this book.

Introduction

Every diner who walks through the door of Ted Brown's restaurant is greeted warmly by the enthusiastic owner. His smile makes everyone feel welcome, but those who know him well understand the satisfaction that adds extra depth to Ted's graciousness. Located on the edge of a revitalizing inner-city commercial district, Ted's restaurant, The Oasis, serves the business community at lunch. The addition of a small jazz band in the evenings has made The Oasis a favorite nightspot for local residents.

Ted's journey toward owning a restaurant had taken almost two years. When he began his venture into small business, what he had going for him was twenty years' experience as a cook, his own ambition, and a fair amount of tenacity. However, because he was an African-American with few financial resources, his ambition had seemed doomed. Now that his restaurant has become a going concern, with pleased customers coming back frequently, it is easy to understand the pride behind Ted's smile.

For several years, Ted had driven past the vacant building where The Oasis is now thriving and felt that it would be a perfect location for a small restaurant. Once, he had arranged a meeting with the property owner, but instead of finding him eager to accommodate a potential renter, Ted was told that he would be required to make a substantial cash prepayment to get a lease. No offer of leasehold improvements was ever discussed. Ted felt terribly discouraged, particularly when he overheard the owner muttering, "You people always have big ideas."

Undaunted, the would-be restaurateur talked about his idea to anyone who would listen, including a banker he knew only casually. That proved to be the breakthrough conversation Ted needed: He was directed to the community development group in his neighborhood, a partnership organization funded by both public and private funds, whose main focus was to encourage businesses and housing that would improve the quality of life in the community. First, the group helped Ted research and plan his business. It then talked to the building owner on Ted's behalf. When Ted next met with the man who was to become his landlord, the discussion had changed radically. Now it centered on the construction of the restaurant, not advance rent. This relationship, although strained in the beginning, has been of great benefit to both parties.

From the days of wondering if there was any chance for an African-American man to start and run his own business, Ted Brown has come a long way. He now has a growing company. Within six months of its opening, The Oasis also began offering catering service in response to customer demand. It hasn't always been easy, but from the smile on Ted's face, you know he thinks it's been worth it.

I understand the obstacles that Ted Brown faced. In more than twenty years of operating my own business, I have met a number of landlords, bankers, and vendors—and even customers—who did not take me seriously or would not treat me fairly, and who were not honest enough to admit that the source of their doubt was the fact that I was a woman. But I have learned to step back from the sexism, decide how serious an impediment it will be, and determine whether it's in my interest to ignore or confront the behavior. Above all, I have learned how to succeed in spite of it.

Up until the 1970s, most independent businesses were owned, operated, and controlled by white men. And the vast majority of small companies employing from 10 to 500 people still have that traditional ownership. Most of the bankers, accountants, lawyers, and corporate executives who interact with the small-business community also are white men, some of them vastly different in attitudes, style, and sometimes even language from the women and minority-group members who are now making their presence felt in the small-business arena. There are those who try to find a common language to create understanding, but there also are those who think we don't belong at all!

A number of challenges confront the courageous souls who aspire to be in business for themselves: The work is hard, the hours long, the pressures are great, and the rewards are sometimes elusive. When racism and sexism are added, an additional hurdle must be jumped. But even with these daunting obstacles, most of those who have done it would do it again if they were asked. The desire to be creative and independent outweighs the prejudice and misconceptions.

If you are willing to make the commitment to creating a new business, if you are willing to learn business concepts and skills, and if you are prepared to invest your own personal time and energy, then money should not be a roadblock. It is possible to find investors and/or loans that can take care of your cash needs. Or you can start your business on a part-time basis and keep your regular job. But you will need to learn new skills; locate good resources; find friends, advisers, and associates who will help. And you will need to enlarge your world.

This book has grown out of my unshakable belief in the entrepreneurial spirit of America and my conviction that a good idea combined with talent and dedication is the most important ingredient for building a successful business. All small-business owners have obstacles placed in their paths, and if you are female or if you are Hispanic, African-American, or from any other ethnic minority, you will face some additional challenges. The best way to meet them is to believe in your own ability to succeed and not let the bias of others undermine your belief. The tough and disciplined path described in this book that will lead to a business of your own will also make you stronger and more creative—two valuable assets for any entrepreneur. They are valuable assets for life as well.

The United States needs new businesses and the new jobs they create. The entrepreneurial spirit inside you, similar to the one that Ted Brown and I share, needs an opportunity to express itself. Here's your chance for a piece of the action. It's a winning scenario for everyone.

1

Start Your Own Business And Hire Yourself

The Possibilities and Challenges Of Small Business

Estelle Archer wasn't surprised by the official company closing notice in her January 1991 paycheck. It was evident that the small retail appliance chain was limping along, and Christmas 1990 had been even softer than everyone had feared. Estelle, the only African-American on the headquarters staff, had started her twelve-year career with this company as an executive secretary. After developing desktop publishing skills along with the word processing aspects of her job, she had created an in-house advertising department that had grown with the company. She designed newspaper ads and had developed a direct mail program that was responsible for the only bright spot in sales over the company's last eighteen months. The company closing wasn't to be complete until mid-May, and Estelle was asked to assist with the "going out of business sale."

In addition to her on-the-job experience in marketing and advertising, Estelle had completed an associate's degree in computer science. Always a self-starter, her first reaction to her employment dilemma was to polish her resumé, pore through the newspapers, and ask colleagues and friends for job leads.

In a few short weeks it became evident that current opportunities were very limited, and future prospects didn't look promising. Finally, her general manager suggested that she consider free-lancing or starting a small business. Taking her usual organized approach, Estelle began to consider the idea. Her first step was to ask the professionals, vendors, and media managers she did business with what they thought of her staring a new venture. To expand her own thinking, she began to spend more time with small-business owners she knew, engaging them in conversation about their work. The more questions she asked, the more she had.

The First Step

Estelle was on target about how to determine if going into business was right for her. Being self-employed is not for everyone, but it is a viable alternative in a difficult job market. And for those who have always dreamed of being on their own, it is the ultimate expression of independence.

The major difference you will find is that rather than look for a position with a company to fill, you will be looking for work that needs to be done and that you can do for a fee. You are not selling just yourself, you are selling your skill. Instead of being hired to do a number of tasks for one company, you will find yourself doing the same task for many companies. Or instead of selling one company's products, you will be selling the products of many companies. Small business is primarily a numbers game—can you find or develop enough customers to create a vibrant business entity?

Your first step is to determine if your idea can become a business. You do that by focusing on three critical issues:

1. Is there a market for the business?
2. Is the work a match for your skills?
3. How much money is required, and can you secure the needed funds?

The Market

Commerce goes on all around us on a daily basis. Regardless of the overall state of the economy, goods and services continue to change hands. The volume of activity for any product or service is known as its "market." The first issue for any potential entrepreneur is to determine how large the market for the planned business is and how many other companies already serve that market. For instance, you wouldn't want to open a pizza shop in a rural community with little traffic, nor would you want to open one where four or five other pizzerias were already fighting for customers.

If your proposed business is a service, your inquiry will be more abstract than if you are determining the market for a product. After you have established exactly what your service is and how it will be offered, call potential clients to learn whether they purchase this type of service from an outside contractor. When you find people who are willing to be of help, ask them about their volume of purchases (if they will tell you) and how much competition there is for the business.

Determining the market for your product or service is a critical first step in your research, so don't take shortcuts. Once you are up and operating is *not* the time to find out that there is no need for the product or service you intend to provide.

Your Own Level of Expertise

When deciding what type of business to open, consider the whole range of your own interests and talents. For Estelle, the choice was easy. During her years in advertising, she had developed a true flair for creating direct mail fliers, and this was the service she intended to provide in her own company.

For some, the journey is more obscure. A Ph.D. in anthropology was motivated to start her own business by her growing frustration at not finding a teaching position close to home. She started a small business in her home doing calligraphy, which she had considered a hobby. Her business really began to thrive when she converted it to a full-service communications firm, providing graphics and writing as well.

If your talent and your market aren't a perfect match, look at ways to make them fit. Can you produce one product and resell others? Can you plan parties and subcontract catering? Can you do electrical work and subcontract carpentry?

On the other hand, if you stray too far from your own expertise, you may encounter difficulties:

Bob Turner was an African-American who had worked as an accounting manager. He had been out of work for almost six months when a friend told him about a small restaurant for sale. The owner wanted to retire and was willing to make an attractive deal. Bob thought it would be perfect—even if he couldn't cook and up until that point hadn't given a single thought to food preparation. Since the current owner had done about 40 percent of the cooking, Bob decided that he would hire a second chef when he took over.

Bob's knowledge gap led to a serious cash flow problem. The purchase deal with the former owner included a monthly payout. This and the salary for the new cook exceeded the salary the newly retired former owner had paid himself. Bob found himself working for nothing. In addition, his lack of experience in buying provisions and using them economically added more cost burdens to his business.

Fortunately, Bob's accounting expertise turned the situation around before his lack of restaurant experience did him in. He became aware of his growing losses early enough to take action before financial disaster hit. His wife joined the enterprise part time as the second chef, and they opened for breakfast to increase overall revenues to cover the cost of the purchase payout. Their first year wasn't easy, but the restaurant thrived after its rocky start. If you play to your strengths in the first place, you may avoid these kinds of trouble.

The Money Requirements

The availability of money is a critical consideration in your early analysis of your potential business venture. You have to project how much financing you will need to get the business up and running and to create a cushion in case of emergency. Do not neglect to consider your own financial requirements, especially if you must support yourself or a family. A new business may not create a cash stream for the first year, and it may be well into the second year before you can draw a full salary. You should match your expectations with your reality. Here is a rule of thumb: A home-based business requires the least amount of capital, although it does entail purchasing office equipment and creating and distributing marketing material. It costs money to let people know that you're ready and able to serve them.

Of course, renting an office, a storefront, or a warehouse takes even more money, so keep that in mind if your idea requires space. Any equipment, fixtures, or inventory that you need will add to the capital requirement. If you require staff at the start, you should have several weeks, or in some cases months, of wages on hand. Again, don't forget to include the money you will need to live.

A seriously underfinanced company starts off at a disadvantage, one that may influence its potential for success for years to come.

Time to Reconsider

Not everyone is cut out for small-business ownership. Being in a job you hate may be a great motivator, but it surely isn't reason enough. Being out of work may lead you to rethink your future, but you still have to want to be on your own and be willing to work hard at it if you are to succeed.

If you have answered the three questions and still find the idea of owning a business appealing, think it through one more time. Consider the benefits, the tough odds, the hard work, and the vast amount of learning still ahead. This is a life-altering decision, and it should not be made quickly.

The Benefits: Why Entrepreneurs Love It

Kari Takashiro spent three months alternating between sending out resumés for a new job in human resources and considering starting her own travel agency. Her former San Diego employer (a defense contractor) had promised Kari its half-million-dollar travel business if she went out on her own, but it was still a tough decision to make after working for other companies for over twelve years.

In June 1991, Kari decided to go forward with her own venture. She started with only herself and a part-time employee. By the end of 1992, her bookings were over $2 million and the agency had four full-time employees and one part-time representative located in-house at Kari's former employer just to service that account. Days are long, and Kari loves every minute of it.

Most of us who have chosen the life of operating our own shops wouldn't have it any other way. The reasons are numerous.

1. *It fosters independence.* There is no one to establish your job duties but yourself. There is no one to establish your work schedule but yourself. No one will accuse you of coming in late, leaving early, or goofing off. Remember, though, that no one will do your work but you—and no one will move the firm forward but you. Your pace, your choice.

This allows you the opportunity to work very hard for many days or even weeks in a row and then, when you are ready to drop, walk away for some rest. This doesn't work for all people and wouldn't be successful for all businesses, but there are possibilities for choice in your own company that you would be unlikely to have if you worked for someone else. If your company grows and profits, you'll know you've made the right choices.

You can wear many hats in your own business—learn new skills and have the chance to try them out. You may discover new talents for analysis, for selling, for managing and motivating other people; you may even find a creative side that you had never explored.

2. *It encourages creativity.* Starting your own business can be the most creative work you can imagine. Now many of the

ideas you've had about what makes a business really work can be put into practice. How the company will look, feel, and act are within your control.

You won't have someone else telling you that your idea for a new product or service won't really work for a variety of reasons you don't believe. You can try out real innovations and find that some of the most out-of-the-ordinary ideas may be the most successful. You can incorporate ideas from customers and vendors to develop new products and services. You can form joint ventures. This is your game.

3. *There is the excitement of competition.* Each and every day that you are in business, you are trying to win over customers and get an order or a contract. If the thought of that gets you motivated, entrepreneurship is for you. You must expect to lose a few along the way, and you can't let that get you down. It's the challenge that starts the juices flowing in most entrepreneurs, particularly when you know you've won because of your own efforts.

The New Challenges

Being in your own business rather than working for someone else requires a change in your perception of yourself, your work habits, and your behavior. Few people go into a venture knowing exactly what it will take and how it will feel to move the business forward to success. The following are four of the new challenges that lie ahead.

1. *You must be able to take risks.* For the most part, you are the one who will be making all the decisions, and you must be willing to do so. Regardless of how much analysis you do, there will always be an element of luck, and that is the risk. For the most part, if you have taken the time to study the facts, the odds should be in your favor. At other times, the outcome will not be under your control.

Risk taking requires a healthy dose of self-confidence. You may not start out completely self-assured, but you must believe that you can get there. As time passes and you make more and more good decisions, your confidence will grow.

2. *You must be a self-starter.* There will be no one in charge but yourself; you set all the rules. Whether you work ten hours a week or sixty is completely up to you, but my experience in more than twenty years of running a small business is that you will work harder and longer when you work for yourself. And the key motivator is that all of the hard work is for yourself. Since the fruits of your labor are your own, that becomes the driving force.

Be prepared to work hard in case of an emergency: If an employee fails to come to work or quits or is terminated, you will most likely have to pick up the slack. The smaller the organization, the more dependent it is on everyone's work, and tasks won't wait until someone gets time to do them. Long, hard days are likely in your future if you want to be successful.

3. *You must complete the work.* If you get bored easily and sometimes leave a job before the loose ends have been tied up, know now that you won't be able to get away with it in your own shop. Unfinished work will sit there undone until it causes you serious problems. There will be no one there to prompt you until it is too late.

There are forms to fill out for every government agency you can imagine, and they must be filed on time. Bills must be paid, and money owed to you must be collected. If you aren't accustomed to this level of attention to detail, be prepared to change.

4. *You must have vision.* Vision is critical for all successful entrepreneurs. While taking care of the current needs of your fledgling company, you must keep your eye on the future and know where you're going and how you're going to get there.

Reading and listening to business news, and talking with other entrepreneurs, can give you a sense of where the business cycle is and where it is headed. You should see how your own company fits into that scene and take advantage of the possibilities while avoiding as many of the obstacles as possible.

Small Business Is Not a Get-Rich-Quick Scheme

It may surprise you to learn that taking as much as a few years to work your way back to the salary you had when you were employed by someone else is considered a success, but this is fairly typical of what you can expect. A new business begins with little or no revenues, and it can take several years before you are bringing in enough money to pay yourself a real salary.

When Kari Takashiro left the defense contractor who had employed her for eight years, her annual salary was almost $40,000. In 1991, she drew no income from her travel business, and in 1992, she drew less than $30,000. However, she expects to reach the $50,000 range by the end of 1994, and she continues to add perks, in addition to the free travel that started almost immediately.

Most entrepreneurs operate businesses that pay them a decent wage and give them the chance to build something to retire on or leave to the next generation. Few really strike it rich, and it would be unrealistic to go into a venture with that expectation. It's an admirable goal, but little else. The attraction is that if you work very hard and very smart and hit the jackpot, it's all yours.

2

Stranger in A Strange Land

Facing a Different Form of Prejudice

It has been more than twenty years since the federal government began assisting and promoting minority-business enterprise. Women-owned businesses were included in many of these programs by order of President Carter in 1978. It would be reasonable to expect some real progress in this period of time, and on some fronts that has happened. There are definitely more women and minority-group members going into business for themselves, but the growth of this sector has been excruciatingly slow.

For women-owned firms, the growth in the number of companies has been dramatic, but the growth in the size of the ventures is not. Census Bureau figures show that although women own almost 27 percent of individually controlled United States businesses, their total receipts are less than 5 percent of the grand total.

The statistics for African-Americans are even less encouraging. Although over 12 percent of the nation's population is black, black-owned businesses are only 3 percent of the total. And while some black-owned firms have grown dramatically large, most are very small and employ few people other than the owner. The environment for minority business is still difficult—in fact, Earl Hord, president of the Pittsburgh-based Minority Enterprise Corporation, describes it as having "grown more hostile over the past ten to fifteen years."

What has changed for the better over these years is the level of visibility of the problems and the openness of dialogue about the solutions. Most of the ground has been broken, and there are forums—conferences, organizations, magazines, and books such as this one—in which to share information and strategies for success. Many of us are absolutely dedicated to helping one another, and you will find information and support now that didn't exist two decades ago. And you will find that you need it.

Whether yours is a new business or a mature one, you will not be able to avoid the racism and sexism that exist in our society. What you experience may be fairly subtle—a sense that you're not being given a fair chance. Or it may be quite obvious—a serious rejection of a fair business offer because the other party does not want to do business with you. These realities will be discussed openly throughout this book. It is also important that you consider this as an issue separate and apart from the general challenge of entrepreneurship and determine whether you have the stamina to fight a thousand and one small battles instead of perhaps a single big one.

In a business of your own, you have the ability to decide how serious the prejudice is and what effect it might have if it continued. You then have the freedom to confront the prejudice or to deal with it in other ways. This is your game; you call the plays.

Finding yourself in a job where institutional bias has kept you from promotions or better work assignments can be frustrating because you have only two options: Stay and fight it out or leave. When you are in business for yourself, you may have to deal with bias on the part of any number of institutions you do business with. You will have four choices for dealing with each situation. Ignore it, confront it, go around it by finding someone else in the organization to work with, or find a new banker, supplier, or landlord to deal with instead. Each of these choices is at best time-consuming, energy-draining, and frequently frustrating beyond belief. Going into business is enough of a challenge by itself, so this added burden can be a serious impediment. If you aren't endowed with a little extra tolerance for the insensitivity of others, patience, the ability to hold your temper, and—perhaps the best defense of all—a sense of humor, you may want to learn these new behaviors. You will need to draw on them from time to time.

Earn Credibility for Your New Business

A new venture without a track record and without a credit history will have difficulty in securing a lease on property or equipment and may face denial of credit. The commercial world relies on past payment history in evaluating whether to open a new account. You can expect to face this regardless of your race, gender, or ethnic background. However, add the institutional racism and sexism that still exists, and the hurdle has just gotten higher. Not insurmountable—just higher. Part of your job will be to identify the obstacles and plan strategies to overcome them. Prejudice comes in so many forms that it is virtually impossible to give a detailed description of how it can manifest itself in every case. Over time, you will learn to identify whether or not it is the dominant issue.

If Your Approach Is Professional, Expect a Professional Response

Start off with the assumption that anyone you approach for a business reason is interested in doing business with you. If you appear unsure of what you want, the response you receive may be less than enthusiastic. The potential vendor, professional, banker, or other service provider may believe that you are just "shopping around" and are not worth their full attention. However, if you have already determined your needs and are fairly specific about your questions, you should expect your interest to be met with a serious response.

This doesn't always happen. You will still run into phone calls that are not returned, material that is not sent, and even appointments that are not honored. At that point, it is important to understand what you are up against. If the individual (or organization) you're attempting to deal with appears to be generally disorganized, that's most likely what's at work here, and things won't get any better over the course of your business relationship. It's tough to have an unreliable business associate, so you should think long and hard about what it would be like to chase these people down every time you need an answer or some service.

On the other hand, a business organization that appears well run and efficient but does not respond to your particular request may very well have a prejudicial attitude about women or minorities. You don't want to look for prejudice everywhere, but you will have to face enough of it to acknowledge the reality. You should repeat your attempts to make contact with the individual or firm in a very businesslike manner; then, if you are still rebuffed, you can assume the worst. Anyone who tries to tell you that this problem doesn't exist has his or her head in the sand.

However, and it is a big *however*; unlike in a job, where you are dealing with one company or one manager, when you are in your own business, you have choices. It's difficult to make the right call every time, but you should be willing to make the choices you have to when it becomes necessary. Entrepreneurship is tricky enough when everyone cooperates. It becomes virtually impossible when you are undermined by someone else's unreasonable bias.

Consider the Effect of Prejudice on Your New Enterprise

In a free and competitive economy, you have many choices to make with regard to the banks, attorneys, accountants, landlords, and suppliers you deal with. But clearly some are better than others, and your company may have many options in some areas and few in others. As a general rule, it is better to walk away from anyone who gives the impression of being difficult to deal with. The only time you need to deviate from that rule is when one option is decidedly more desirable than the others.

For example, if you want to open a clothing store and your attempts to secure the rights to an important line of clothing have been met with stony silence or suspicious questions, you may still need to forge ahead for the good of the venture itself. Or if a location is perfect and the landlord makes unreasonable demands on you that let you know that there is a lack of respect or trust, it may still be important to try to work out a lease to give your fledgling business the benefit of an advantageous place to begin. These are tough judgment calls because the cost in time, effort, and extra aggravation can far exceed the value of what you get.

If you feel you must try to carve out a business deal with someone who seems resistant, do so in a very professional manner. There are four steps in doing this.

1. *Document what you are experiencing.* Keep track of the dates and times you've attempted to make contact or the questions or requests that have gone unanswered. Put this in writing, and send it directly to the individual involved. The fact that you are keeping this record may wake the person up.

2. *If the gentle reminder doesn't succeed, send a copy to the person's superior with a letter.* Don't be accusatory, but rather, express your lack of understanding as to why this person wouldn't want to respond to a valid business proposal. It won't win you any popularity contests, but it may get you the attention you need and deserve.

3. *Meet with the person involved.* Face-to-face confrontation is very effective, but only for those who can handle it. Never try it in the heat of the situation because anger renders you less effective. If you feel that you've been wronged, organize your evidence, then schedule a meeting and present this evidence in a strong manner, demanding an explanation. Your goal is to intimidate if possible because this will level the playing field in the future.

4. *Consider pursuing a legal course of action.* If the offending

party is a bank and you can document discrimination, you may have a case under the fair credit laws that have been enacted by Congress over the years. Lawsuits are time-consuming and emotionally and intellectually draining, and you don't want to become involved in one without due consideration of all the issues.

As long as there are differences between people, there will be those who act badly. Laws won't change them, although laws will curtail their behavior. Public opinion may put additional pressure on them. When you start out on a business venture of your own, you have enough to accomplish without these impediments. But they are there, and you would do well to pay attention; avoid these unreasonable people and organizations if possible, and do not let them discourage you. Hopefully, the day will come when they will learn that it is in their economic self-interest to overcome prejudice.

3

Get Your Bearings

Finding the Education And Information You Need

It would be a serious mistake to allow a lack of formal education to prevent you from becoming an entrepreneur. The majority of white men who have gone before you did not, and some have succeeded beyond their wildest expectations. In fact, Dave Thomas, the founder and CEO of the Wendy's fast-food restaurant chain, just received his high school diploma in 1993. And while his story may be one of the most prominent success stories of a self-taught entrepreneur, it is far from unique. The over 10 million owners of independent American companies include both Ph.D.s and high school dropouts. Where creativity and hard work are the defining issues, lack of formal education should not be seen as a barrier. In fact, education and training may be the one area in which women and minorities have a genuine advantage.

For those considering a business of their own, acquiring new skills is both necessary and desirable. Operating a business involves a number of different skills, including managing people and managing money and other assets. Your instincts about your own company will improve over the years, but you should try to begin with enough basic information to make good decisions, particularly in the early phases when you are more vulnerable.

Universities, community colleges, and various government agencies offer many programs exclusively for women and/or minority entrepreneurs. Even if you have limited financial resources, you can still acquire the training that will enhance your potential to be a successful entrepreneur. Costs can range from virtually nothing to several hundred dollars for a seminar covering more advanced skills.

How then do you find the right course for you? Start off by asking yourself the following questions:

- Do I understand the overall concept of entrepreneurship? Am I skilled mostly in one specific area?
- Do I learn more easily in an intensive day-long or even week-long course, or do I find it easier if I can take time between classes to study and work on my own?
- Am I most comfortable with people who are ethnically and racially similar or of the same gender as myself when I am in a new learning situation?

Ask yourself this last question very seriously because you have the choice of where you go to train and you want to maximize the impact of this training. If you are not at ease in the course environment, you won't learn as well.

Courses to Consider

Overviews

If you are looking for a substantial overview of entrepreneurship, one of the best investments of time and money you can make is a $25, one-day, prebusiness workshop sponsored by the Service Corp of Retired Executives (SCORE), which operates within the Small Business Administration (SBA). It covers the basics of financing, record keeping, types of business organizations, taxes, and insurance along with marketing and business planning. The one-day format does not allow any topic to be covered in depth, but you will be able to determine the extent of your existing knowledge and skill on each subject.

Then you can decide how and where to proceed to expand your knowledge base.

A number of women and/or minority business associations and local development groups offer overview courses that have four or five sessions with several offerings for each session. For example, at 9 A.M., there might be panel discussions on getting a loan, principles of marketing, writing a business plan, and running a restaurant. At 10:30, four more courses would be offered, and again at 1:30 and 3:00. Some topics may be repeated; many will be presented only once. This allows you to choose the four that are most important to you and avoid sitting through those that are of no interest. Panel discussions offer a variety of views and can be more interesting and spirited than a single instructor. Also, the panels are often made up of current small-business owners, and their experiences can be very relevant. The cost can range from $75 to $150 for the day, including lunch and a chance to network informally with others.

Many universities and community colleges offer semester-long courses titled "How to Start Your Own Business." If you're anxious to start a business right away, a three- or four-month course may take too long. But the benefits of in-depth study will outweigh the time if you feel unfamiliar with financial management, marketing, or other specialized business topics. Since each topic is given at least one full class, work will be slower and more comprehensive, and there will be time for you to read and study between classes. This learning experience is far more complete than that a short course can offer.

Ongoing Education

As you begin your new business venture, you will uncover a number of areas where you thought you had a working knowledge, but where your information was incomplete. This is where ongoing education comes in.

For some of these areas, a few hours or even part of a one-day course is not enough to cover the material.

• *Financial administration and cash flow management.* Do you know how to set up a record-keeping system for tracking all receipts and expenses? You may have a basic knowledge of bookkeeping that is sufficient to carry you through the early days, but once you begin to hire employees, a number of reports and tax returns will need to be filed with federal, state, and local authorities. Your profit and loss statement is a source of both tax and management information. You will need to understand these documents well enough to interpret them as a measure of how you are currently doing and what mid-course corrections are needed. You needn't become an accountant, but you should understand finances as they pertain to your business.

• *Sales and marketing.* Do you understand the difference between the two? Marketing is how you promote your company and its products and services, and how you know who your customers are and how to reach them. Sales is the actual transactions between business and customers. But of course, they both are far more interesting and complex than that. Developing a strategy for your particular business and bringing it to life could easily require a full semester of work.

An additional area of the marketing field is public relations, which can include ideas on how to get your company name in front of the public as often and positively as possible. You may also want to learn what to do if you become the focus of bad press after a product failure or accident.

• *Human resources.* Once you have begun to hire others to work in your business, there are personnel management issues and labor laws to consider. Do you know how to motivate others or what to do about a problem employee? There are a number of legal requirements, and you should learn what they are.

• *Other skills.* Quality management, promoting good customer service, and a fairly new theory of peak performance have been presented in various learning formats, from one-day courses to semester-long presentations. You may also need to learn such skills as computer programming or improved public speaking.

Running a business of your own will challenge you on all levels, and you will need and hopefully will welcome the new learning this occupation involves. If you allow yourself to become complacent, your business will lose its vitality.

The Best Learning Environment

You are learning new disciplines, new skills, and new behaviors, and it is critical that you find the best class for you—one that suits your learning style and makes you feel comfortable enough to participate and ask questions. Since so many organizations are involved in entrepreneurial training, there is a wide variety from which you can choose the best, most cost-effective environment for you. Here are organizations you should be contacting, along with other sources of information that you may find useful.

- *Local colleges and universities.* The advantage of this learning environment is that the course work is designed by professional teachers who know how to structure a class in a logical and organized way. This may make some of the tougher topics easier to understand. There will be books and other written material that will give you a chance to follow up on your own. Many of the technical topics can be best learned here.

The disadvantage for some may be the cost. Other than the for-profit seminars, these may be some of the highest-cost classes offered. It is not unusual to see a two- or three-day small-business course sponsored by a university priced between $400 and $600. Since every dollar counts to a start-up, keep the cost-benefit analysis in mind. Also, courses are seldom taught by business owners with hands-on experience. In the wild world of entrepreneurship, theory and practice are sometimes at odds. Fairly often, what *should* happen *doesn't,* and most owners accept that fact as a reality and learn to adjust quickly.

- *The partnership between academia and government: the Small Business Development Centers.* Small Business Development Centers (SBDCs) are sponsored by the SBA and housed on the campuses of universities throughout the United States. The activities promoted by the various centers differ, but all provide a certain amount of actual education in the form of seminars given in a one-day or one-evening format over a period of a few months. The topics are fairly timely, and the centers use both their own staffs and local business owners. And while their own staff members are professors and theory-oriented, they work with so many small businesses that they are aware of the more unusual problems faced on a day-to-day basis.

The other main function of an SBDC is giving individual counseling to small businesses that request it. There are a number of different formats, and it can prove to be of valuable assistance.

■ *Federal, state, and local governments.* Agencies at every level of government are interested in business and job creation and carry out a number of efforts to encourage this activity. Education is just one of these areas, but it is something you should know about because the cost is often low and the reward is great.

The SBA/SCORE prebusiness workshop is by no means the only training in which the SBA is involved. The SBA works with organizations other than the SBDCs to cosponsor workshops and seminars. Training is a major function of the SBA, and you should call and register with it as early as possible. Once you are on the SBA's mailing list, other agencies can pick up your name and forward information on their own offerings.

A number of other federal agencies are actively involved in encouraging, developing, and training would-be or early-stage entrepreneurs, most notably the Department of Commerce, whose mission is the promotion of business. It sponsors workshops on a variety of topics, including "How to Export," a subject of great interest to growing manufacturers. There may be a Department of Commerce office in your town to call; if not, you'll want to get in touch with the Small and Disadvantaged Utilization Office at the Washington, D.C., headquarters of the department.

There are two other places you can go for information. One is the Government Printing Office Bookstore, located in your closest Federal Building. It has an entire section on small business, and several well-priced books are available. Also, for the price of a call, you can get your senator or congressperson to do some research for you. Each has a staff that is usually happy to answer any constituent questions, and when it comes to helping a new business get started, you will find a cordial response.

This process is repeated on the state and local levels. Call your state, county, or city department of commerce or development authority first and find out what activities it is sponsoring. Use your state and local politicians for this effort as well. The more local the office holder, the more interest he or she has in developing business because it provides jobs for voters. You might find a council member or an even higher elected official showing up at your grand opening for a great photo opportunity.

- *Organizations such as the National Association for Women Business Owners or Minority Enterprise Organization.* A number of nonprofit organizations have developed and support courses for new business owners. These courses are created by the local board, and the actual sessions are usually taught by experienced business owners who are members or supporters of the organization.

Classes can vary from a one-topic evening meeting to a day-long session that covers a variety of topics and may have two tracks, one for the new owner and one for the more experienced entrepreneur. You will be taught by peers who understand your experiences and frustrations and may be able to warn you of the effects of the prejudice you will inevitably face. These leaders are also willing to share their own creative solutions. These may not be "by the book," but the information will be practical and usable. And the environment may prove more encouraging to you as you watch other women and/or members of ethnic and racial minorities reach out for the challenge that "going on your own" provides. Regardless of how you decide to receive the balance of your learning, it is worthwhile to try this out.

- *For-profit seminar producers.* There are some very excellent seminars given by private consultants and speakers on a variety of business topics, although most of these programs are for the more experienced business owner. As you would expect, both the promotion and the presentation are fairly well produced in order to attract paying customers and build future audiences. There are courses on human relations, such as "team building" or "dealing with a difficult employee." There are courses covering sales and marketing, including how to create a direct mail or telemarketing campaign. Recently, a number of courses about developing "quality" programs in business have been making the rounds.

A wide array of technical seminars, from cost accounting to desktop publishing, are also offered, and most will add to your skill level or your overall ability to manage your business into a growth phase.

Some for-profit seminars are competitively priced, but most are fairly expensive. Prices may run as high as $800 for a two-day workshop. However, there will usually be good value in the material.

▪ *Potential suppliers.* Your new vendors may be a good source of free or low-cost learning. A particularly good supplier may show you how to use its product or service as well as helping you to understand how it fits into your overall business goal. You should expect this additional service from your attorney and accountant and from any advertising or communication firm you have under consideration. A professional who doesn't have the time or inclination to work with you to make sure you're an informed client won't give you the service you need. Make information a part of your expectation.

A number of large companies, such as IBM, the regional phone companies, and AT&T, sponsor seminars for small-business owners. The cost is usually low. The range of topics will vary: limited in the case of IBM (specific software applications) and fairly comprehensive in the case of the phone company. These workshops are provided to create good public relations for the sponsor and as a marketing tool for the sponsor's products.

▪ *Your customers.* Most new entrepreneurs aren't aware of what a valuable source of information their potential customers may be. On an informal one-on-one basis, they may give you ideas about the products they buy, the service they require, and how they choose vendors. This marketing information is free and very valuable to you. Ask questions and use the answers.

If your potential customers are "big" business, the learning may be more formal, more valuable, and still free! Virtually all large U.S. corporations do some government business and are required to establish a formal subcontracting program with small and minority businesses; some of these programs include women-owned businesses and some do not. These programs solicit participation in the bidding process as well as provide education and guidance to nontraditional entrepreneurs in an effort to level the playing field. Make an appointment to see the small- or minority-business representative, and while discussing sales opportunities, ask about other "in kind" assistance the company may be providing.

One of the best vendor training programs is sponsored by Conrail (Consolidated Rail Corporation), which operates a 12,800-mile track system in fourteen states in the Northeast and Quebec, Canada. Its subcontracting program began in 1976 and has grown through its sponsorship of trade fairs, informative publications, and training, including team building and problem solving. In 1992, it purchased products and services worth over $100 million from minority- and women-owned businesses. On top of that, if your company becomes a supplier to Conrail and you are not able to transmit paperwork through an Electronic Data Interchange (EDI) system, Conrail will assist your company on a one-to-one basis. Could a supplier ask for more? You may be able to find other equally proactive customers.

If You're Selling to the Government

"How to Do Business With the Government" seminars are given throughout the United States, normally sponsored by a federal government agency in conjunction with state and local government. The SBA, the Department of Commerce, and the

Department of Defense have been the primary conveners of these procurement workshops, but other agencies have also participated. They have two formats going on at the same time. One is a series of "how to" classes that cover a number of topics, including how to fill out a bid, how to get paid in a timely fashion, how to finance a government contract, and how to institute a "Quality (TQM)" program. The other is a trade fair where the buyers staff the booths and where sellers (hopefully that's you) can make a pitch for their products or services. This is a great place to make a number of business calls in a short period of time. All you will need is some quality printed material to leave and your own enthusiasm.

Consider All the Possibilities

As you can see, the education you receive before you go into business is only a small part of the information you will need in order to make your venture a success. Encouraging business development is a mission of many levels of government and a number of educational and social organizations as well. Open yourself up to the possibilities—it's well worth your time and effort and may go directly to your bottom line.

4

A Winning Game Plan

Making Your Business Plan A Road Map for Success

For the sophisticated and experienced entrepreneur, a business plan is a document used primarily to secure financing from banks or investors. To be sure, most loans for new businesses need to be secured by other assets, and few women or members of ethnic minorities who are just starting out have enough equity to be bankable. However, it is still very important to take the time and effort to create a working business plan.

As a new entrepreneur, the primary use of your plan should be to analyze how you will go about making your new venture come to life. The document should spell out all the elements of your business and provide a step-by-step strategy to make the company a reality—a way of measuring your progress during your first year of operation. It is important that you revisit and revise your plan as your business matures in order to review your progress and set new goals.

A business plan is also a good tool to use when discussing your thoughts and ideas with friends and associates. You will find that the questions and suggestions of others will give you additional ideas on how to refine your original strategy.

You can also use your finished plan to introduce your business concept to potential landlords, vendors, and bankers. Until you have something more tangible to show others, such as products, a catalog, or your opened shop, your plan will give a view of how your idea can grow into a company. Make it as complete as you can.

The Basic Elements

The six basic elements of a business plan are:

1. The concept
2. The market
3. Operating strategies
4. Capitalization
5. Sources of revenue
6. Financial projections

Each element must be fully developed, with all the details investigated. The language should be straightforward so that the idea of the business is clear.

The Concept

Explain in full detail exactly what product or service your business will offer. Whether your product is a basic one that everyone uses or cutting-edge technology, your explanation should be full and complete. Consider these questions as a starting point: What is it? Where will you get it? How will you sell it? Why would anyone need your product or service? Why buy it from you? Why are you qualified to offer this product or service?

As you write, think of yourself as a customer and fully develop the reasons why you would do business with this new company. Be a tough customer—if you can't convince yourself, how can you expect to attract others to your new enterprise?

After the first draft of this part of your plan is complete, you should show it to your friends and other business people and ask for their input. Listen to what they say.

If you are not totally convinced that your idea has success

written all over it, now is the time to modify and revise—*not* after you get into business.

The Market

Who are the customers you expect to attract to your new company? How many potential customers are out there? Where are they buying now? Why will they change to you? How much money do they spend on your product or service? How much of this money do you expect to attract?

These six questions are the core questions any new entrepreneur needs to answer. You must know who your potential customers are, how many of them there are, where they are meeting their needs now, and why they would change to you. The total amount of money spent is the total market. Your share is the projected size of your business.

1. *What is the size of your market?* If you are planning to open a children's clothing store, you would begin by estimating how many children live in the area covered by your store. How many households are there? How many children in each household? If there are 12,000 families near your store and each has 2.3 children, the total number of potential customers is 27,600. Next, estimate the clothing purchases per child. If this is $250 per year, the market in your area is in excess of $6 million. Half of these potential customers probably shop at the mall. This leaves $3 million of business that your new business can compete for, and that's an exciting prospect.

Finding the information you need to determine the size of a market is not as difficult as you might think. Whether you are selling to other businesses or to individuals, there are formal counts available through local or state government offices. Each municipal taxing authority has a list of homeowners and can tell you the number of households. School districts collect information on the number of school-age children. Chambers of Commerce have data on numbers of businesses and professionals. Regional development authorities also have valuable demographic information. If you plan to sell into a national market, you can get information from companies that sell mailing lists. By reading their catalogs, you will find the total number of companies in each category, and this gives you an estimate of the total number of potential customers. This is the first step.

2. *What is the average sales per potential customer?* For most goods and services, this type of information is available through government agencies. Many universities study business trends and release this type of data. There is someone somewhere studying almost anything! You can also get the data you need by doing a survey of your own. Call at least 10 percent of the potential customers you can identify, and ask them direct questions such as: How much do they spend on a product annually? Where do they buy it? How often? Their answers will allow you to create your own estimates. If you can afford to pay for research, there are a number of marketing firms that can conduct a study. This is a fairly expensive proposition—it could cost more than $10,000.

3. *How much of the available business will go to you? And how long will it take you to get it?* Be realistic. Established companies have relationships and habits on their side, and you will have to break through that with promotion and enthusiasm. You can take some customers from competitors and also develop new ones.

With the information you have gathered, the formula to determine market share is

$$\frac{\text{Number of customers} \times \text{sales to each}}{\text{Percentage of market share}} = \text{Your volume base}$$

As I described earlier with the clothing store example, this information will help you decide if your venture is feasible and also give you goals for your first few years.

Operating Strategies

This section is where you describe how you plan to launch your business, where you expect to locate, how you expect to market your goods or services, and what ideas you have for competitive advantage. If your hot idea is home delivery of groceries or other products that are not usually delivered, mention "a new concept of customer service." You don't want to give away all your secrets, but you do want to show that you have thought through what it takes to get a business from the idea stage to the planning stage to the operating stage.

If you have made arrangements with potential vendors to carry a hot new line or to offer special financing, here is where you describe that fact in detail. If you have formed strategic alliances with other companies or negotiated with individuals to represent your product or service, describe those opportunities. Anything you have been able to work out to enhance your business belongs in this section.

Capitalization

The two key questions addressed here are:

1. How much money do you need?
2. How will you get it?

Money is the lifeblood of any company—if you have less than you need, your chances for success are limited, and a good portion of your time will be spent trying to find more instead of operating your enterprise.

How do you estimate your needs? There are several elements:

- *Capital to establish a place of business*
  - Preparation of space
  - Machinery and equipment
  - Marketing material
- *Inventory and raw material*
- *Working capital*—At least six months' worth of overhead expense (rent, utilities, wages), and preferably one year's worth

(Text continues on page 41)

Figure 1. Preliminary version of a business plan.

Business Plan
Safety Exchange, Inc.
August, 1989

Concept

Liquidating excess inventory has long been a profitable business in the retail marketplace. Off-price outlets, catalogs, and TV shopping networks have been utilized to reach customers for disposition of available product.

Industrial products present a different scenario, however. Distributors of industrial goods, such as safety clothing and equipment, cannot easily merchandise their excess product in a cost-effective manner. Most sales are achieved without advertising and, in many cases, without utilization of a central store. Therefore, even the presentation of excess product is a problem. Returning excess inventory to a manufacturer for credit triggers a 25 percent restocking fee and, in some cases, the loss of future quantity discounts.

Safety Exchange has developed a unique method to address this market opportunity. Safety Exchange has designed an Information Network to broker excess inventory to interested buyers. Listings of available excess inventory are mailed or FAXed to subscribers on a periodic basis. Additionally, Safety Exchange broker/salespersons actively pursue all sales opportunities. The integrity of Safety Exchange will be guaranteed to the industry by dealing only with the distributor, never the end user.

Safety Exchange initially will begin operations with three office locations: Western Pennsylvania, Maryland, and Connecticut. These initial offices will be located in existing offices of company officers in order to maintain a low-overhead operation. The financial resources of Safety Exchange will be primarily directed to maintaining a state-of-the-art computer system as well as to direct marketing efforts.

Extensive marketing and sales efforts will position Safety Exchange as a proactive player in the industry. Listings of available excess inventory will not be merely passively sent to subscribers. Safety Exchange broker/salespersons will maintain personal contact with subscribers and let them know when excess inventory that matches their needs becomes available. A marketing goal is to have distributors consider the Safety Exchange Information Network as a backup extension of their own normal in-house inventory. Distributors should consider the Safety Exchange Information Network a supply source capable of delivering product faster than original manufacturers.

The Safety Exchange concept can also be applied to other markets, thus providing natural opportunities for business expansion. The first logical extension of business will be to use the Safety Exchange Information Network to serve the safety clothing and equipment manufacturers themselves. Manufacturers can use the Safety Exchange Information Network to sell their excess and second-quality goods while maintaining their normal channels of distribution. When desired by the manufacturer, the origin of the goods can be kept confidential and not disclosed to the buyer.

An additional expansion opportunity will be to apply the Safety Exchange concept to general industrial suppliers. Almost any industrial marketplace is a logical target of opportunity for application of the Safety Exchange distribution concept.

The attraction of the concept for investors and stockholders is the absence of the problems associated with the production and distribution of a physical product. Safety Exchange is a pure service business. Expansion opportunities are extensive and will not require substantial capital investment. Low fixed costs will support increasing profits during the high-growth period.

The four principals of Safety Exchange bring a unique blend of talent to this venture. The CEO, Suzanne Caplan, has twenty years of experience as a safety clothing manufacturer and has extensive industry and product knowledge.

The president has twenty years of experience as a systems engineer, having worked for the Burroughs Corporation, Westinghouse Electric Corporation, and Digital Equipment Corporation.

Safety Exchange is well prepared to take advantage of the latest in computer and telecommunications technologies to apply a revolutionary distribution concept to the safety industry.

The Market

The safety equipment and clothing business generates $2.2 billion in annual revenue through approximately 6,500 independent distributors nationwide. Virtually all distributors are forced to inventory far in advance of requirements by "just-in-time" delivery demands. With a constantly changing industrial environment, excess inventory has grown to 3 to 4

(continues)

Figure 1. Continued.

percent of total volume, or over $70 million. Since most end users are very specific about their needs, liquidating unused inventory within a local market area is difficult to accomplish, although these same products may be in demand in another market area.

Safety Exchange was created to facilitate the sale and exchange of excess inventory between independent distributors in different parts of the country. Safety Exchange offers this service to the selling distributor at a cost less than the traditional 25 percent restocking fee charged by most suppliers for merchandise returns. The advantage to the purchasing distributor is immediate delivery of goods at below-market prices. The Safety Exchange Information Network is an ideal way for purchasing distributors to satisfy their customer requirements and for selling distributors to reduce their excess inventory burden.

By the end of its third year of operation, Safety Exchange forecasts a membership of 1,000 companies, or 15 percent of the market potential. Sales are projected at $3.5 million, or 5 percent of available inventory.

Additionally, Safety Exchange expects to be introducing technical database services and custom software during the third year.

Operating Procedures

The initial marketing task for Safety Exchange is to register safety distributors as Information Network members. Distributors registered with the Safety Exchange Information Network can participate as both buyers and sellers of merchandise. Revenues will be obtained in this process by charging for registration and subscription access to the Safety Exchange Information Network.

Distributors will be charged a one-time processing fee to register their companies with the Safety Exchange Information Network database. Information such as company name, location, product lines and types, and quantities needed will assist Safety Exchange in effectively serving its customers' needs. Although a customer may not have a product to list for sale on the network at the time of registration, this process entitles the company to subscribe to Safety Exchange Information Network services for the purpose of both purchasing inventory and assuring quick access if it wishes to list its excess inventory for sale at a future date.

When distributors join the Safety Exchange Information Network, their contract documents will include a copy of the current commission fee schedule. Commission rates range from 5 to 10 percent depending on the dollar amount of the transaction. Smaller transactions have a higher commission rate.

From information provided by the distributors, Safety Exchange creates a computerized inventory database which serves as the basis for periodic mailings of an Inventory Bulletin to Information Network subscribers. The primary information supplied by the distributors for inclusion in the Inventory Bulletin is items such as type of product, condition of product (e.g., whether it meets code specifications), and quantity of product available. Secondary information, when available, will include crucial industry information that could affect the distributor's business. Information such as tax laws and national and international events can be used to inform the distributors while also stimulating business for Safety Exchange. Availability of the Safety Exchange Inventory Bulletin is a function of the subscription level paid for by individual distributors.

Safety Exchange offers three levels of subscription service. Level A consists of Inventory Bulletin mailings at least fifteen (15) times per year. Level B consists of Inventory Bulletin mailings at least twenty-six (26) times per year. In addition, Level B customers will receive special notification mailings and/or telephone notification of new merchandise that becomes available between regularly scheduled mailings. Level C consists of Level B service transmitted by FAX instead of first-class mail.

Safety Exchange will focus on service and maintain constant contact with its Information Network members by including a locater service. This service will be organized in such a way that when new merchandise is entered into the Information Network database, a list of distributors looking for that merchandise will be automatically generated. For example, if XYZ distributor is looking for particular merchandise on a steady basis or in a particular situation, Safety Exchange will be able to provide the service of notifying that distributor when the merchandise becomes available for sale on the Information Network.

Financial dealings will be structured in such a way as to protect all parties involved. Safety Exchange will maintain an escrow account in which all sale proceeds will be deposited prior to the shipment of goods. Only after goods are shipped by the seller and checked and approved by the buyer will the funds be released to the seller, minus commissions payable to Safety Exchange. Our goal is to protect buyers by ensuring that they receive the correct goods and quantities in the stated condition before the funds are released to the sellers. Sellers are assured of payment in a completed and approved transaction because the funds are held in escrow for that purpose. Control of the funds will assure receipt of

(continues)

Figure 1. Continued.

commissions by Safety Exchange and minimize the need for accounts receivable.

Once a selling transaction has been completed, Safety Exchange will forward complete shipping documentation, including labels, to the selling distributor. Goods will then be drop-shipped to the buyer. On some occasions, Safety Exchange will take goods on a consignment basis; on rare occasions, Safety Exchange will consider the outright purchase of goods.

Capitalization

	1st Year	*2d Year*
Capital required	$12,000	$ 6,000
Marketing material	6,400	4,000
Office/phone	12,000	15,000
Travel	7,200	7,200
Postage/supplies	4,800	4,800
Salaries—secretarial	6,000	10,000
Officer salaries	0	36,000
Commissions	0	12,000
Total	$48,400	$95,000

Officer Investment:

Year one: 1,200 shares @ $50.00	$60,000
+ revenue	15,000
Year two: 1,200 shares @ $50.00	$60,000
+ company revenue	50,000

First year loss projected at $33,000.
Second year loss projected at $45,000.
Third year profit of $24,000.

Sources of Revenue

1. Distributor registration fees
   One-time charge of $125 to be entered into the Safety Exchange Information Network database. Permits unlimited listing of merchandise for sale.

2. Subscription fees, annually at 3 levels
   a. Receive Inventory Bulletin via mail 15 times/year
   b. Receive Inventory Bulletin via mail 26 times/year as well as special mailings and/or telephone notification
   c. Receive level B via FAX

Level	Subscription Fee ($)	Expected User Distribution (%)
A	80.00	20
B	125.00	30
C	150.00	50

3. Commission fees on sales, 5–10% based on value
   a. Less than $1,000, 10%
   b. Between $1,000 and $10,000, 8%
   c. Greater than $10,000, 5%
4. Technical database user
5. Custom software sales

Financials [*not included in this example*]

___

The total of these items is the sum of money you will require.

You should have a good idea of where you can take your plan to secure financing before you complete this section. As you successfully secure the money you need, update this part of your overall business plan to reflect money on hand.

Sources of Revenue

This is where you describe how you expect to charge for your service or product. Will you charge by the hour? by the job? on an annual basis? Will you charge based on estimates? or on a cost-plus basis?

As you complete this section, think through how soon revenue will come into your company and consider ways to bring customers in the door as soon as possible.

Your banker, your investor, or anyone who sees your plan in order to make credit decisions should be able to see exactly how your business is going to generate profits. Since you return money to lenders or investors from profits, this is the area of their greatest concern.

Financials

Making financial projections is rather complicated, and this is where a good accountant can be of real help. The goal is to project the revenues and expenses of your company for its first three years of operation. The numbers for the revenue side will come from the market projections you made earlier in the plan. You can get a fairly good handle on the expense side by adding your rent, utilities, other monthly overhead charges, and salaries. Remember that these figures will not stay the same—sales may be up some months and down others. Expenses may be heavier some months also. You can predict when you might be earning a profit and when you will need extra cash to grow.

There are some easy-to-operate software programs (called spreadsheets) that will aid in the preparation of your financials. They allow you to plug in any fixed numbers (rent, phone, and so forth), then work on the numbers that change. Your accountant probably uses these programs and can teach you how to use them.

In 1989, I formed a new business with three other partners for the purpose of brokering excess inventory among safety equipment distributors. To our knowledge, this type of business had not been tried before, so we had to explain why we thought it would work and how we expected to transform the idea into a business. Figure 1 shows one of the early versions of our plan.

We spent four months working out all the details of this plan. It was important that all three partners agree on the various strategies to be used, fees to be charged, and goals to be met. We then spent six months market-testing the idea. When we found that some of our concepts did not work, we worked through the plan again. Few businesses are exactly what their founders thought they would be from day one. Less than a year after we began, we rewrote the whole plan to reflect the realities of putting our concept into practice.

Although you can hire a consultant to create a business plan for you, I recommend that you do it yourself. This is your business, and you must be the one to create it, think it through, and set goals that you believe to be realistic. After all, you are going to be the one responsible for making them happen. Remember, the more time you take to plan in advance, the less time you may spend trying to figure out what went wrong.

5

Attorneys, Accountants, And Consultants

Finding the Best Advice and Advisers For Your New Business

Before you decide on a legal structure for your company, before you give new venture a name, before you sign a lease for space, and before you sign any agreements for loans, you will want to find an attorney and an accountant to give you good advice. These are issues that will come up early in the life of your business, and they require the use of good professional advisers.

Your company will want to register its name and its legal structure with the appropriate state government office. Filling out the forms is not difficult, but making the decisions may be. Whether your business is a sole proprietorship, a partnership, or a corporation has legal as well as financial and tax implications. Some of the considerations are as follows:

- Will you want to raise money from outside investors?
- Will you show early-year losses that you will want to use as credit against future profits?
- Do you have other personal assets or business interests that you want to protect from any liability resulting from your new venture?

- Is there a complicated partnership arrangement in your venture?

If you take the SCORE prebusiness workshop (or another one like it), many of these issues will be raised. You may even have some tentative directions that you expect to follow. But it is always safest to review these decisions with both an attorney and an accountant to make sure that your specific needs are being met. A competent professional will also help you decide what your future needs will be and help you structure and plan your business to accommodate those requirements as well as your current needs.

Your lawyer should also review any leases you are considering and perhaps suggest special clauses to reflect arrangements you may have made with your landlord. Loan documents or investment agreements should also have a legal review before you sign them.

Your accountant will be able to give you advice on setting up your bookkeeping system so that the information you record will be accurate from the first day. You even need to track the money you spend to set up your business because that will be a deductible expense of your company. You want to pay no more than the taxes you owe on your company's profits. A good accountant will earn his or her fee. Take the time and make the effort to find good professionals, and you will be repaid in many ways over the years.

Finding the Best Attorney and Accountant

Friends or associates who have started their own businesses are your best resources for finding a professional referral. Don't ask just one person, and don't just ask for one name. Lawyers and accountants are not all equal, and they do not all specialize in the same areas. Your concern at this time in your business life is to engage a cost-effective professional who will consider all aspects of your current and future plans and recommend the best way to structure the company. The most expensive firm in town will probably give you accurate advice, but at a high price.

Always set up a preliminary meeting with any professional you have under consideration *before* you make any commitment. Come prepared with a list of questions, and make sure you get complete answers. This first meeting should be free, so don't expect to get specific advice about your business. Rather, you are seeking information on the individual's background and expertise. Does she have special expertise in your industry or business type? Ask about his hourly rate, and also get an estimate of how many hours will be required to accomplish the tasks (incorporation/tax returns) you anticipate at the moment. Is a retainer (money in advance) required?

By engaging in serious, albeit brief, consultation with your potential attorney or accountant, you can get a feel for the working relationship you may be able to develop. Mutual respect is very important at this juncture. You will be taking advice that has serious implications for the course of your venture. If you don't feel comfortable, move on to a new candidate.

Getting Value From Professional Advisers

Attorneys and accountants bill by the hour, and most lawyers charge in increments of 6 minutes, or 10 percent of one hour. A casual phone call can run up a $100 charge, so it is prudent to be careful about wasting time. However, if you have a document to be reviewed, a contract to be negotiated, or a thorny financial problem, don't hesitate to get good advice before you create a situation that costs two or three times as much to undo. I once signed an informal lease without specifying that I was signing on behalf of my company, and a dispute over the tenancy cost $1,000 to correct. One call and I would not have been so casual.

To save money, be prepared before any call or visit with all the pertinent documents, and plan all of your questions in advance. Not only will you keep your cost in line, you will get better information if you consider exactly what answers you need.

Obtaining Additional Outside Advice

Most lawyers focus on specific areas of the law, and even those who work in a general business practice can't have total expertise in everything. You should expect to be referred from time to time to other professionals who have special knowledge (copyrights and patents, for example). Sometimes you may go out on your own to get a second opinion. If you are not completely confident about the advice you are getting, by all means seek additional consultation. You are the one who is responsible for the actions of your company, not your advisers, and you should be assured that you are on the right track.

If at any point you have the feeling that your attorney or accountant is not responding to your needs, it's time to take action. If your calls are not returned or extensions are always being filed instead of tax returns, you aren't being properly served. Remember, you are the client, and you are paying the bills. Find someone who values your business. It is also important to find an adviser who treats you with respect—never accept one who patronizes you in any way.

Contacting Professional Consultants

You can find professional consultants who will help you write your business plan, create a marketing strategy, design a corporate logo, develop a software system, write a personnel policy, and assist with a variety of other business issues. Many have corporate backgrounds and established themselves as independent consultants after cutbacks at one or even a series of previous jobs. (In fact, this may be the type of business that you are planning.)

Expertise has a price, and the cost can vary greatly, but all consultants charge an hourly rate, normally ranging from $50 to $175 an hour. The time is not kept as strictly as a lawyer's but it can still mount up quickly. Much of the work you might be able to do on your own, but technical, graphic, or other highly specialized work can easily be outsourced to an independent. You pay only for the work and the time you need. And there are no additional employment costs.

Choose a Consultant Carefully

Simply because people may call themselves experts does not mean that they are. Check samples of previous work (graphics, for example) or talk with previous clients before you engage anyone to do work for your company. Ask for at least five referrals, and make sure you actually call each one to get more than a single opinion. Since you can expect a consultant you are considering to give you the names of only satisfied customers, do a little digging of your own. Ask previous clients if they know of others who have used the individual in question. You may get names you didn't already have, and you should follow up on these leads also.

What You Want to Know

- Was the work satisfactory?
- Was the project (or series of tasks) completed on time?
- Was the original estimate accurate?
- Were there many add-ons (items not covered by the original agreement but necessary)?

Regarding add-ons, be aware that they not only can greatly delay a project but may cost more than the original project. Avoid anyone who has a history of this.

When you engage a consultant, establish the terms of your agreement as specifically as possible—in writing and in advance. Make sure that the nature, scope, and expected result of the work are understood by everyone involved. If you are looking for custom software, for example, the developer should understand all of the functions you require and agree that your system will have that exact capability. If the project is a marketing plan, remember that writing the plan and implementing it are two separate issues.

Since consultants charge by the hour, time is also money.

When you discuss how many hours the project will take (the cost), you also want to establish a time frame for the completion of the project. If the software is a twenty-five-hour project at $100 per hour, the total cost should be approximately $2,500. If the consultant works four hours per week, this would take six weeks; that is probably not acceptable to you, so you'll want the consultant to agree that the work should be completed in two to three weeks. If time is critical, determine a penalty for lack of completion and try to get it into your contract. Many consultants require you to pay a retainer in advance to assure at least a part of their payment. This is fair, but don't pay anyone unless you are convinced that the work will be completed satisfactorily. Because consultants have expertise in specific areas, it is possible to get professional assistance in a very cost-effective manner—just remember that you have to manage the consultants, not the other way around.

Finding Free Help That Works

There are a number of places you can go to get one-on-one consultations at absolutely no cost. You may not get the service of an office visit at your location, but you can find real value if you look for it. The three main providers of assistance are:

1. SBA (primarily SCORE)
2. Universities (SBDC)
3. Community development corporations

SBA/SCORE

At each regional office, the SBA has a minority business development officer and someone designated to oversee programs for women entrepreneurs. The minority program usually has a counseling component, with technical assistance available to individual businesses. Few women's programs are that extensive. The SBA's SCORE program provides much more than the prebusiness workshop. The real heart and soul of its work is a cadre of dedicated, primarily retired business executives who donate their time to work with new and upcoming business owners. No one can question the generosity of the participants, but the quality of the advice can vary greatly from one city to another and even from one individual volunteer to another. The key here is in the match. If you find someone with the expertise you require, your business will derive substantial benefit from the genuine interest and counsel he or she provides.

However, because SCORE uses volunteers, it tends not to reject anyone who feels that he has something to contribute. A small number of its members simply aren't equipped or have knowledge that isn't current enough to benefit your company. If you are assigned to someone whose advice does not seem to be relevant to the matters at hand, gracefully exit without wasting your time and energy. If the thought of this makes you uncomfortable, perhaps you should look elsewhere before trying SCORE.

Small Business Development Centers

The next stop would be the Small Business Development Centers (SBDC) housed at many major universities. The SBA is one of the sponsors of these centers, and they provide a number of services, including individual counseling. Here is a chance to meet with a business school faculty member to discuss your particular business problems and learn what alternatives you might have for solving them. This is a great source of free advice, with time being the only limiting factor. There are only a few instructors to meet the needs of a number of business owners, so you will not have a long-term relationship, but many seemingly thorny issues can be corrected with some knowledgeable advice.

Through the SBDC or a university business school, you may be able to become the subject of a student study project. In some cases, the students would be undergraduates, but it is also possible to become a case study for a group of MBA candidates. Their work won't provide instant answers to specific questions, but the report you receive at the end of a semester can be the equivalent of a $10,000 independent project, and yours came for free.

A student-directed market survey is particularly valuable because of the time and energy required to review demographics, check out competition, and question potential (or existing) customers. And it is likely that those being interviewed will be more candid with a student because they are trying to be helpful. If yours is an interesting business concept, you can find some real help at a college or university.

Community Development Corporations

The final resource for free business consultation is community development corporations. These organizations are brimming with information and assistance for any potential business owners looking at their communities. You must be considering a specific area, but if you have already found a location, by all means check out the CDC for that neighborhood. Although a CDC is not a loan granter, it is a source of information for virtually all government and private loan programs available. Staff members are happy to match your business with potential funders. The role of CDCs in financing is discussed further in Chapter 6.

Most CDCs have one individual who is a business developer, loan packager, and/or technical assistance director. I thought I was aware of most available services, but the extent of this resource was one of the most pleasant surprises I found while researching this book. I spoke with individuals who were able to help a potential entrepreneur complete a business plan, find a business loan, secure a location, plan an expansion, and do anything else that was needed to contribute to the success of a new business in the community. They work with "would-be" and "start-up" entrepreneurs as well as with existing companies. A number of the business incubators were started by these technical advisers. I found them easily accessible, knowledgeable, and eager to help.

Any successful business needs good outside advisers. You can hire some, find some for free, and even create a board of directors to give you feedback. Much of what you go through in the early days is frustrating but typical. It helps to hear this from others and to get objective feedback about strategies for success.

6

Other People's Money

Financing a Start-Up

A number of difficult tasks confront any entrepreneur before a business opens and during its operation. One of these (and it is *only* one) is how to finance both the start-up and the ongoing company. Your goal should be to secure regular bank financing for your business once it is operational and has established a track record. However, it is highly unlikely that your venture is bankable in the early stages. There are two exceptions.

One is for those who have enough equity in other assets (normally a home) to qualify for a second mortgage. This type of loan also may require an income other than that from the business you are starting, such as the salary from a part-time job or the income of a spouse. The second is a program for those who are not qualified for a traditional bank loan. They can receive loans guaranteed by the Small Business Administration. These loans are processed through the banking institution, but 75 to 90 percent of the risk is assumed by the SBA. Typically, these loans are for existing businesses, but there are times when special emphasis is put on loans to female or minority start-ups. Check this out; if you are starting your business at the right time, it could work out well.

If you can't go to the bank, where can you go? There are a vast number of other ways to finance a new venture. Here are ten ideas to consider:

1. Credit card cash advances
2. Leasing rather than buying equipment
3. Family and friends
4. Barter
5. Vendor credit
6. Partnership with another company
7. Local development authorities
8. Minority loan programs
9. Micro loan programs
10. Peer lending groups

These are all bootstrap ideas that will probably provide only part of the financial needs of your new venture, so that you may have to use more than one of them to raise the total amount you require. Each one has its own benefits and problems. Be careful when combining several; the terms and payback requirements must be compatible. Here is a synopsis.

1. *Credit card cash advances.* The appeal here is that credit has already been approved and securing the money is almost instantaneous. You may already have thousands of dollars in available credit through several bank cards.

Payback begins immediately, but it can be stretched out over several years. Using this cash to start up is not a bad idea, but it is also constructive to leave a little in reserve in case you have an emergency need down the road.

2. *Leasing.* The purchase of machinery and equipment can be a big cash outlay for a new business. Even if you are able to finance a purchase, you must raise a substantial down payment. Not so with most leases. You will still have monthly payments, but other than a security deposit, up-front cash requirements should be minimal.

The downside of this arrangement is that you have no ownership in the equipment to show for your regular payments. However, many leases have a buy-out provision at the end of the term.

3. *Family and friends.* The first decision you must make is whether to ask for money in the form of an investment or a

loan. This decision is based more on personal considerations than on anything else. In fact, most decisions governing your business transactions with friends or members of your family are more a reflection of your relationships with them than purely objective business decisions. If you are close to others who support your effort at independent business and can afford to advance you some money, they may welcome the chance to help. If you have a particularly clever concept that is expected to bring a good return, a small investment could yield a healthy reward. Even a loan at an above-normal interest rate could be a good deal for both parties.

Be as businesslike as possible to avoid any misunderstandings at a later date. Draw up a written document that describes in clear language exactly what type of arrangement you have negotiated. For the protection of both parties, have an attorney review the agreement. Caution in the beginning can prevent animosity later on.

4. *Barter*. You may be purchasing a certain amount of goods or services from other small businesses. The product or service that you intend to provide may be of interest to your potential vendors. For example, Linda Virenza's new Italian restaurant needed a good advertising campaign to let Pittsburghers know that a great new neighborhood bistro was now open. She was able to have a clever audio spot produced, but she had limited resources left to buy air time. Several radio station managers agreed to accept free meals in return for running the ad. The campaign was a hit, and Linda continued to do business on this exchange system. Some of the credit was used by on-air personalities, and that added excitement to her venture.

There are a number of barter exchange businesses operating that formally enroll members and track credits earned and credits used. You'll find them listed in your local Yellow Pages.

5. *Vendor credit*. Each of your vendors will have its own credit policy, some more liberal than others. A portion of your start-up money will be spent with various types of vendors. If you have a good personal credit history or an existing relation-

ship with a supplier, you may be able to get credit that will reduce your need for cash. Don't be afraid to ask.

As an example, if you are starting a retail operation, inventory will be a major start-up requirement. You might ask if you can take a portion of the merchandise on consignment—that is, the ownership of the merchandise remains with the supplier, who is paid when a sale is made. This is another way to reduce the need for start-up cash.

6. *Partnership with a mature company.* Your business idea may have grown from the need of an existing company or have been developed to fill the small orders that a larger business no longer wishes to handle. That company may well end up becoming your largest customer because you can do the work that it still requires. And your company will be more economical because of your lower overhead costs. Explore the possibility of getting financial assistance or free or low-cost services from your business association.

Large industrial companies will help to set up subcontractors who can do small segments of a larger job. These formal programs may include both business and financial assistance. The downside of this arrangement is that your company becomes almost a captive of the larger business. Unless you can expand beyond that relationship, your company will be vulnerable to the whims and conditions of your prime customer.

The assistance you secure may be in the form of free rent, and that can make a real difference. Carolyn Taylor, an African-American woman, started a graphic arts business in Philadelphia as an adjunct to a large commercial printing company. Her rent was free, and she had the use of their sophisticated computer systems, also at no cost. In return, Carolyn did not charge for the work she did for the printer and brought all of her own clients as new customers to the printing company. The space was available and the computer time was unused, so it was a good deal all around.

Look for these strategic alliances; they can be a source of financing, free services, and an immediate customer base.

7. *Local development authorities.* A development authority is

an organization that has as its goal development of various sorts, including housing, recreation, and business. It is a department of your city and/or county government, and most likely a revolving loan program is included among the services it provides. Almost all have a special interest in including women and minorities in their programs. Your idea and business plan will have to be well developed by the time you approach a development authority, and you may need some personal assets to use as security for a loan. It is certainly worth a call or a visit.

There are also organizations known as community development corporations that limit their interest to a single neighborhood and are involved in the arts, housing, and public safety as well as business. Only a few of them have actual loan programs, but most have business development directors who can help you put a loan application together and find the best program to secure funding. Many of these community groups are funded in part by nonprofit foundations, and in some inner-city areas, they will make an actual investment in a new company. Chapter 5 covers the other services CDCs provide.

In Philadelphia, a community development group founded by the city's Hispanic clergy assisted a local black entrepreneur in finding a location to start a launderette that was needed by the community. Each city has its own group of activists, and it doesn't hurt to call around to the local Chamber of Commerce or church council. Most of the grass-roots groups get little press, so you will have to go directly to community and church leaders to ask what special initiatives they have for small business.

8. *Minority loan programs.* Every large city has at least one minority enterprise group, and some have several, funded by different sources and having different goals. While they seldom acknowledge it officially, few have any real interest in working with Caucasian women. It is an ongoing question whether white women qualify as a minority for many of these programs, beyond just the loan aspect. Keep that in mind before you waste a good deal of time.

If you are a member of a racial or ethnic minority, you'll still want to ask some serious questions before you begin any application process. The most important is what minimum loan figure is of interest to the group. If you need only $25,000, the group might not feel it worth their while to package such a small loan. The minimum I have heard most frequently is $100,000. It would be fair to ask how well these programs are meeting the needs of the minority community when they deny the mid-level credit required to start smaller businesses. Some of that need is being filled by special minority-directed programs within development groups.

The application and loan processing cycle of the enterprise groups is fairly long—perhaps six months or more from your first contact. If your concept requires quick movement to make it work, don't count on this being an answer for you.

9. *Micro loan programs.* Filling the need for very small loans, those between $1,000 and $2,500, is an innovative new loan concept: the micro loan. It is directed only at start-up businesses and is meant for those without good credit histories— those not typically bankable at any level. Most of these programs are targeted at both women and minority business enterprise.

The money originates from government development organizations, but it is passed to community groups for administration and loan-granting authority. Many use a peer group lending model to develop the program. Other aspiring or beginning business owners form a committee whose role is to decide which applicant gets a loan; they also must make sure that the loan is fully paid back. The available loan money cannot be lent to anyone else until the original borrower pays it back. This is an incentive for both caution and assistance on the part of the group. Call your development authority and ask if it has funded any micro loan programs.

10. *Peer lending groups.* The micro loan peer lending groups were modeled on the private peer lending that has gone on in some ethnic communities, particularly Asian, for a number of years.

Business owners (or in some cases those wanting to be) form a small organization to both create a loan fund and give one another general business assistance. Each member contributes a fixed amount of money each month, which forms the source of capital to lend. A group of twenty can create a fund of $10,000 if each puts in $100 per month for only five months! New money continues to be created, and as loans are repaid, the money can be lent to other members.

The major benefit of such a program is that it includes the advice and interest of other members of the business community. The group wants its members to succeed so that the available loan money will continue to grow and the money out will come back. It's a winning proposition for everyone.

There may be other programs that are unique to your type of business, background, or area of the country. Just because you aren't eligible for standard bank financing does not mean that you are out of the game. It requires resourcefulness to get into and stay in business for yourself.

When Sherry and Thomas Caldwell decided to open their own office cleaning business in Rochester, New York, they used half of the available ideas and thought about several others. An African-American couple who both held other jobs in the early stages of their venture, the Caldwells put together a bare-bones budget and found several sources of capital. The initial projection looked like this:

Equipment

Truck or small van	$14,000
Industrial floor sander, sweeper, carpet cleaner	6,500
Office equipment: desk, phone, PC	2,100
	$22,600

Supplies

Stationery: business cards, business fliers	$ 1,200
Cleaning supplies: rags, soap, cleaners, solvents	1,800
	$ 3,000

Direct Labor Expense

4 employees × 1.5 months @ $900 month	$ 5,400

Overhead

Rent for office, 3 months	$ 1,500
Phone lines, etc.	600
Manager salary, 3 months	4,500
	$ 6,600
Total Capitalization	$37,600

Facing the need for nearly $40,000, the Caldwells almost gave up the whole idea of a business. Then they sat down with a small-business developer and came up with the following ideas:

1. Lease truck and cleaning equipment	original total	$20,500
Down payment and three-month lease		4,400
	savings	$16,100
2. Purchase used office equipment and use old phone systems	new cost	$ 500
	savings	$ 1,600
3. Offer three months free cleaning to company that would do free printing	savings	$ 1,200
4. Use home office and hire only part-time manager	savings	$ 3,000
5. Count on personal credit card cash advance for some of labor expense until revenue comes in	savings	$ 1,500
Total Savings		$23,400

Now their total start-up cost was $14,200, which was far easier to reach. A family member made a $7,000 loan, and a friend added $5,000. The rest came from Sherry's savings. The dream became a reality.

A large number of very successful businesses have started on little capital. Some, like McDonald's or KFC, have become legends. Even Apple Computer started out in a garage. Your investment of human capital can leverage a small amount of cash into a successful business.

7

The Care and Feeding Of Your Local Banker

*Finding and Working Successfully
With a Bank*

Entrepreneurs who have a strong relationship with their bankers have a secret weapon for their businesses. Even though you may not be able to find your early financing at a bank, try to develop a relationship with a banker as soon as you can. The more familiar you are with one another, the more you will utilize the valuable services of your bank.

Jim Williams is an African-American contractor. One of Jim's earliest business contacts was Tom Nunnally, thought of by many Pittsburghers as one of the city's most astute small-business bankers. Tom helped Jim to successfully bid on contracts, finance them, find qualified subcontractors, and organize his business operations. At one point, when Tom was in transition between banks, he even went to Jim's office on a regular basis to provide advice and encouragement. They are friends, and Jim has learned from this friendship. Tom has learned things too and has created a loyal bank customer.

It is a popular misconception that the sole purpose of the bank is to make loans. Banks are far more than just a source of capital. If you view your bank solely as a place you go when you need financing, if that's the only time your banker sees you in person, you are unlikely to develop a very successful banking relationship.

Your banker should be a primary source of information for you. A good banker will keep up with the general trends in the economy and specific opportunities within your own business community. He or she will know and should be sharing with you what companies are moving into the neighborhood, which companies are doing well and anticipating growth, and which are heading for financial trouble. This information is valuable to your ongoing business and any business expansion you might be planning. After all, if a new plant is starting up within blocks of your business location, don't you want to be the first one in the door offering your goods and services?

Good bankers spend part of their day enlightening their customers about the bank's capabilities. The information offered will range from the various ways in which the bank can structure a loan to how it can help you to invest your excess capital so as to earn the best interest rate. Banks now provide more and more services to their customers. Most VISA and MasterCard authorizations are issued by a bank, and the bank is responsible for handling these charges and remitting the money to you, the vendor.

For a company that bills its customers directly, the bank may provide a lock box service, which means that money is paid directly into the bank; the money is available faster than it would be if the funds went to you and you had to take them to the bank for deposit. Estate planning for yourself individually, pension planning for the employees of your company, and a vast array of other services are also offered by banks, depending on the individual state's banking laws.

Finding and developing a good banking relationship requires work on your part. Start by doing research to determine which bank will meet the needs of your business. Ask other business owners you know about their bankers to find out which banks are the friendliest to the small businesses in your community.

Some of the concerns you might have are:

- Does the banker take a personal interest in her accounts?
- Does he work to structure loans to meet the particular needs of his customers?
- Is she willing to ease terms during times of temporary difficulty?
- Is he knowledgeable about other aspects of small business and willing to be an adviser to his clients?

Also, make sure that the bank you are interested in is in good financial shape. A troubled bank is an erratic lender and may deny or call loans because of *its* problems, not yours.

What Type of Bank Do You Need?

The structure of commercial banking continues to change radically. Financial problems in the banking sector have forced many small banks to merge with larger and better-capitalized institutions. This means fewer choices for the potential customer. You will want to seek out a bank that specializes in small business. If you have a number of choices in your community, you will want to look for a bank that specializes in the type of business that you operate. You may find articles linking the growth or expansion of a company with a particular bank in the business section of your local newspapers or in any business periodicals that cover your community. Also, examine the ads that the banks run and the types of financing deals each bank frequently pursues. This will give you a better picture of exactly what the bank is interested in and how customer-friendly it might be.

It is also possible to find a highly specialized bank, that is, a bank owned and operated by a particular group and serving primarily that community. Although they are not numerous, there are African-American–owned banks, Hispanic-owned banks, and banks that are owned and operated by women. If you feel that you would be more comfortable with one of these specialized banks, you can locate them by calling your local business association or the state banking authorities.

Finding the Right Branch

Most regional banks use a branch banking system; that is, they have a number of small offices in various locations. But not all offices serve the same market. Some are directed at the individual consumers, others are retail oriented, and still others are directed at a special business sector or serve a general business clientele. For example, in my hometown a number of the banks have branches in a downtown office building that houses many law firms. These banks are geared to serving the escrow accounts that many lawyers maintain, transferring funds and disbursing them when required. This would not be the right branch for a small manufacturer to choose. If you have started a small manufacturing firm, you want a bank whose loan officers are familiar with the financing needs of a business that may need to borrow money when a particularly big contract is being produced. It may be necessary to lease equipment when you can't finance a purchase, and not all banks offer this service. A bank located near an industrial park where small manufacturers operate is more likely to offer these and other services geared to meet your particular need.

On the other hand, if you operate a small retail business in an area and there's a branch of the bank right in your community, this bank will most likely be serving many of the stores in your locale. It might offer a night depository, which would not be necessary for lawyers but might be a valuable service for you, enabling you to deposit the day's cash receipts after you close in the evening.

Finding a Bank That Needs You

All federally chartered banks operate under a vast number of regulations, including one called the Community Reinvestment Act (CRA). While the terms are relatively general, the spirit of this Act is to make sure that banks invest at least part of the money that they take in deposits from the local community back into that community. The purpose of the Act is to prevent banks from taking money from a community and investing it all in another state or another country, therefore, starving the local area of the capital it needs to be vital. In addition to the federal auditors monitoring the CRA, you will often find local officials—the mayor or city council—scrutinizing the lending practices of a particular bank in your area. From time to time you'll see articles in your local newspapers about these audits being done and banks being either praised or chastised for their performance in community reinvestment. Pay attention. Once in a while the bank may be put on the defensive and forced to solicit loan business in the local community.

If a bank located near you that you already have under consideration is coming under increased pressure from the CRA, it will be looking for you. You can provide it with business investment in the local community that it can point to in its report. If your business is one that creates jobs, that's even better for the bank. Sometimes the bank needs you more than you need it.

Meeting Your Local Banker

Your bank is not merely an institution, it is the individual who represents it, so you must find the right person with whom to develop a working relationship. Don't hesitate to make an introductory call. Either stop in at the bank or call and set up an appointment with the branch manager. Even if you're only at the point of opening an account, this is the individual on whom you're going to depend for the services that your company will need down the road, so you want to identify the best banker your company can find.

At the first meeting you'll want to get a reading as to whether it's a good personal match. Does the manager seem friendly and want to spend time with you, or does she keep looking at her watch or taking phone calls and interrupting your meeting? Is the manager genuinely interested in you as well as your new business? Or is she only answering the questions you ask or selling the services of the bank to you and your business? Do you get the feeling that this branch manager believes you're going to develop a business that in the long term is going to be a profitable account for her bank?

Banks as institutions have worked very hard to operate without prejudice, but they can't control the bias of everyone who works for them. I have known bankers who are sexist, and I have known bankers who are racist, and anyone who believes that this isn't a reality or a fact of life is living in a dreamworld. But at this point, your job is not to change attitudes but to find the best bank and banker to help your small company grow. So if a banker exhibits some prejudice, patronizes you in any way, or treats you with less than complete respect, simply turn on your heel and walk away. It is worth the drive to another bank to find the right banker for you. Waiting until the day you need help is too late.

The factors that make up the right fit are not easy to define. My best and worst experiences with bankers were both with white males of about the same age. I prefer to find a woman in my age range with a similar background, but of course, this isn't always possible. I have learned, however, to be cautious enough to check out my current manager with other women business owners. Add your research to your instincts. The point is that the banker you choose is someone you're going to get to know well; choose a person with whom you believe a relationship is worth cultivating.

When You Meet Your Banker, Share Your Dream

Before you get down to opening your business account, you will have already developed your business plan. When you go in to open your new account, take your plan with you and leave a copy at the bank for your file. Sell your business to your banker as if he were a customer. Explain how you got involved in the business, and explain what sorts of plans and dreams you have for your business. Make your banker as enthusiastic about your prospects as you are.

You can do other things to make your business dream come alive. If you're producing a product, bring a sample. If you have a catalog or brochure that you give to prospective clients, bring it too. Any tangible information you can give to a banker to let him or her know that you are serious about your creation will benefit you in the long run.

Invite Your Banker to Lunch and Do a Little Show and Tell

If you're thinking about a retail business, small manufacturing plant, or suite of offices, you may want to show this to your banker. Invite your banker to lunch, and then afterwards take her on a tour of your proposed business location. Make your written plan come alive. Describe how you expect to set up your operation and what that will require. Show that you know how this business operates, who the customers are, and how you're going to reach them. If there is room for expansion at that location (room in the back to build another building, or additional rooms in the building that you might take over), walk through that space (if possible) and explain how your company can grow at this location, eliminating the need for expensive moves. Make the future come alive so that when the time comes to fund this aspect of your growing concern, your banker will be able to visualize it.

There are many things you may need from your banker in the future or services that the bank can provide. Even if you're not close to asking for any sort of line of credit from the bank, it can run a credit check on a customer before you extend credit and get stuck with unpaid bills. A banker can make your deposited funds available to you a day or two sooner rather than after the standard three-day wait. And there may come a time when checks will cross in the mail and you'll be momentarily overdrawn. A banker with whom you're familiar will authorize the payment of a check and hold the check for a day or two. A banker who does not know you is unlikely to do this.

Getting a Loan When You Need One

Money is the fuel for a small business. You will need it to purchase inventory, pay your workers, and buy the machinery and equipment you need to expand your business. Even if you start out with an investment or your own capital, the day will come when you need to borrow money to expand. You will need to rely on two things: the working relationship you've established with your bank and a loan proposal that really sells.

What's in a great loan proposal? It should begin with information on the history of your business concept, and then answer the following questions:

- When will you begin, what are your goals, and how do you expect to achieve those goals?
- How will you reach your target market?
- What are your sales targets?
- Have you uncovered potential problems, and how do you expect to deal with them?

The first section of a loan proposal will answer the following questions:

- What exactly will the money be used for? If it is for new equipment purchases, include data and quotes for the machines.
- What assets will be used to secure the loan?
- What payback terms are requested, and what profit flow will be used to satisfy these terms?

The second part of a loan proposal is the financial records. You should include a balance sheet showing your assets and liabilities, including those that are personal. If your assets are machinery and equipment, enclose a separate list identifying the various pieces of equipment or machines that you have. Include their current market value. If you have fairly high accounts receivable (money owed to you), bring an itemized list of these accounts and how long the money has been outstanding. You may be able to borrow against these accounts.

And finally, you'll need to do some projections. What do you expect your sales to be over the next one-, three-, or five-year period? What do you expect your expenses to be over that same period of time? And what sort of profits do you ultimately expect to show? If your banker hasn't taught you how to do a pro forma statement, go to a class to learn how to do it or get your accountant to work on one with you. The format is the same as the one you use to report your current business results, but the numbers are estimates of how your business will change in the future.

What your banker is going to be looking for is whether you will have sufficient profits to pay back the loan. And what you should be looking for when you prepare the statement is whether you can use the loan to make sufficient profits to make it worthwhile. It's never a waste of time to put together a loan package. Even if you never apply for the loan, you will learn a valuable lesson about your business.

The Best Approach When Applying for a Loan

There is an old saying that "banks only lend money to people who don't need it." For the most part this is true but misunderstood. A business that "needs" money is usually a business in trouble. To a banker, this is a risk, and bankers don't like risks. You need to understand their job and how they are rated by their superiors in order to fully comprehend why they behave the way they do.

A branch manager is responsible for bringing revenue and profit into the bank, and making loans is a way to achieve these goals. However, when a bad loan is charged off, it reflects on the record of the banker who made the loan. So even if you think to yourself, "It isn't his money," remember that it may be his career on the line.

The best approach to enhancing your chance of getting the loan is to make your banker feel that the loan you are requesting will be secure. It's not that you "need" money to survive, but rather that you require money to grow. Your application will tell the banker how you expect to use the capital to increase profits in order to pay back the loan.

If you see an expansion in your future, give your banker as much advance notice as possible—let her know that in six months or one year she can expect you to arrive with a loan application in hand. Your banker will be convinced that you have thought through both the present and the future of your company, thus making you a good risk. The bottom line is that even if you need the money, you don't ever want to make this obvious.

And last, be prepared to negotiate the terms of your loan. Interest rates represent the return to the bank, and they are partially based on the level of risk. You will have to be flexible and be willing to pay a slightly higher rate if your business is new. Remember that it is possible to renegotiate to a lower rate once you have developed a track record.

Keeping the Lines of Communication Open

Once you've been successful in closing on a loan, you should not stop paying attention to your banker. There are continuing informational and financial services that she can provide. But there is an even more important reason to keep in touch. Most banks require periodic review of any outstanding loans, and the more information your manager is able to maintain about your company, the easier it will be for her to write up a review of your account. This will make any banker happy.

When your accountant gives you a quarterly statement, give the bank a copy for its files. My experience with bankers has been that they love paper. The bank examiners require documentation, and most bankers will feel safer if they have more than they actually need. In addition to the reporting, it is equally important to schedule regular meetings to discuss the results and review current loans and future financing needs.

If you find yourself facing some short-term difficulties in the near future, the time to discuss the possibility with your banker is before it happens. If problems are known in advance, they will not alarm the banker. Whether it is being a few days late with a payment or paying only the interest and deferring the principal, your banker can make adjustments to help you over the short term.

Bankers Hate Surprises

There are few things that bankers hate more than finding out that a borrower is having trouble after one or more loan payments have been missed. At that point, they have fewer options than they might have had before cash became short. You'll put your banker on the defensive if you aren't forthcoming and candid with him. Not only will your credit suffer, but what may have been a very constructive relationship with your banker will be damaged, and this can be very costly to you and your business. Any banker with experience understands that business has cycles. Bankers expect customers to need assistance. What troubles them is finding this out from a delinquency report rather than from the customer.

Bankers Are People, Too

Your banker is just another working person with a mortgage and debts and perhaps a family. Few earn what would be called generous salaries, and the job can be very tedious with few rewards. Many people get upset over financial issues and feel that bankers aren't being fair, putting the blame on the banker for what are strictly held policies of the institution. While an individual branch manager has some independent loan authority, there are always a loan committee and bank auditors keeping tabs on his or her operation.

Good bankers are good salespeople. The product they are selling is money, and frankly, if they don't sell any, they won't make any profit. Money is your life blood and their commodity. But just as you want to sell your product for the highest price *and* you want to get paid, they have to bring back the best return and also get paid.

At times, every banker has had to institute collection actions, which may include foreclosure of property and garnishment of wages. It isn't easy to enforce these procedures, and few bankers are insensitive to the difficulties of their troubled customers. The scene of the mean old banker gleefully evicting a widow and her children just isn't true, although it probably accounts for some of our discomfort around bankers. Most bankers find any of these harsh actions painful to deal with and have empathy for their customers. They would much rather be cautious about a loan before it is made.

The bottom line is to look past the money that is involved and see your banker as an individual and a valued member of your own business network.

Using a Second Bank

A good banker will tell you that one full-service bank is all you need, but a great banker will recommend that you use two banks—one for backup. If you have very little cash when you start, this isn't a good idea, but somewhere down the road, when excess cash does become available, the time will be right to look for your second bank.

If your bank merges or is sold to a larger institution, it may change its philosophy and decide to focus its activity, including its lending, at certain levels or in particular business sectors. If your company is not in the area of business category chosen, you may be denied the capital you need for reasons that are totally beyond your control. This may happen gradually, but in the case of a bank sale, it could be relatively sudden. If your line of credit is up for review at the time that changes are taking place, your loan could be suddenly called or your line of credit canceled. There won't be time for you to go out and find a new banker, and your whole business can be put in jeopardy. With a backup banker, you have a place to go.

Don't just put your money in an account and leave it there. Repeat most of the process discussed earlier in this chapter and get to know banker number two on at least a casual level. You may not have time for the "lunch and tour," but drop off information about your company to make her more familiar with your operation. You never know when this backup banker may be your last line of defense.

When the Bank Stays but the Banker Is Gone

I once had a particularly good relationship with a branch manager that lasted several years, and it never occurred to me that she would leave. When she finally moved on to greener pastures, I did nothing. I continued to deposit my money and make my payments and cash my checks, nodding occasionally to the new manager. Months passed and I stopped sending updated materials for the bank's files and basically lost contact with my bank. What a mistake! One day the new manager called me, saying that the bank needed a current statement and that he wanted to discuss my account. I prepared my papers and scheduled a conference. The meeting went okay, but we sure didn't hit it off personally. When I left the bank, I felt as if a member of my team was gone—and all through my own negligence.

If your banker leaves, find out as soon as you can who the replacement will be. Schedule a visit and decide as soon as possible whether the replacement is as good as the original. If not, follow your banker to a new branch if possible or find a new branch to which to move your account. It is worth the effort; it is worth the drive.

The bottom line is that business is a team sport—employees, customers, suppliers, and bankers all play. Find yourself a talented banker and you're on the way to a winning season!

8

Good Intentions

Are Set-Asides and Special Programs for You?

A good business needs good customers, and it is important to learn which potential customers represent the best long-term prospects for your company. You probably won't have the time or the money to conduct a major marketing program, so you will want to focus your attention where you will find a friendly response. If you have an industrial product or service and plan to focus on larger companies, you may find a lot of competition. However, to assist in the process, many of the large publicly traded corporations and institutions are reaching out to minority- and women-owned businesses. Some of the programs are driven by a sense of fairness, some by the need for good public relations, and some by the requirement of government contracts.

Set-Aside Programs

In the early 1970s, Congress passed a series of laws and regulations that required most government contracts to include a provision that the "prime" (named) contractor must utilize "small and disadvantaged" businesses as subcontractors. The regulations in some government agencies were written specifically for minorities, and in some instances required a specific percentage of participation. In 1978, President Jimmy Carter signed an executive order that included "women-owned" businesses in the process.

The theory behind these laws was that when public (tax) money was being spent, all citizens should have an equal right to compete for contracts, and that minority- and women-owned companies needed special assistance to secure a fair share of the opportunities. Most Fortune 500 corporations do at least some business with government agencies, and virtually all responded by creating a new position within the purchasing area for a developer to find and utilize minority- and women-owned businesses as suppliers. Many business successes have been created through these programs.

The automotive companies have taken a particularly strong position in minority purchasing programs, responding to both requirements of their government contracts and sensitivity to their commercial market. Ford's Minority Supplier Development Program has had some outstanding successes in identifying potential vendors and then taking an active role in assisting them to grow and prosper. Dave Bing started Bing Steel, Inc. in Detroit in 1980. In 1985 he began a relationship with Ford that resulted in the auto company's brokering an agreement between Bing Steel and a larger Canadian company to form a joint venture called Superb Manufacturing, which Bing operates. This new concern was doing $20 million with Ford alone by 1991.

Ford takes a genuine interest in the continued success of the vendors it helps to develop and offers seminars and other ongoing one-on-one consulting. Each year it hosts two forums that bring together the auto companies' top management and minority-company CEOs. This helps cement the working business relationship. They work on projects together.

For those able to fit into a set-aside or development program, there is great opportunity. But this opportunity is limited to a small number of vendors. In fact, companies that had 100 percent white male vendors prior to 1970 will almost cease developing new minority suppliers when their total gets to 10 percent of purchases. Why not give women and minorities a chance to be the majority of vendors? After all these years, the issues are still controversial.

There are some potential pitfalls in your company's focusing most of its efforts on participating in the corporate minority purchasing programs:

Karen Ortiz registered her Hispanic–female-owned Massachusetts-based industrial distributing company with sixteen prime contractors in her first four months in business. This took 75 percent of her time, but she felt the rewards would be there. She worked on this track for over seven more months in 1990 and finally was successful on an order exceeding $20,000. In the next two years, her subcontracting business grew to almost $300,000, representing 60 percent of her total of half a million dollars in volume. The poor New England economy, defense cutbacks, and aggressive competition from other suppliers has cut that number by two-thirds in 1993, and her total sales will not exceed $220,000—a serious drop that threatens her whole enterprise. Karen didn't take enough time to build a diverse business base, and she didn't consider that the set-aside contracts could be as volatile as the general economy and that the loss of one major account could undo a year's hard work.

My own experience with soliciting prime contractors was all frustration and little success. After Carter's inclusion of *women-owned*, I began an aggressive campaign to market to government contractors, most of whom were natural customers for the products we manufactured. I started out with a mailing, followed up with phone calls, and even went on trips to the other side of Pennsylvania and as far west as Seattle and Hanford, Washington. The small-business developers were very positive about opportunities, but it was impossible to convince the actual buyers that we deserved a chance to at least quote on some orders. They were not interested in making a change.

I spent almost a year repeating the process and achieved zero success. Then finally I thought we had a breakthrough—we were invited to bid on an annual contract for welders' gloves. This was our real strength, and we were the only manufacturer bidding on a direct basis. Surely our prices would blow everyone else out of the water! They did, but we did not ultimately get the contract. We were disqualified for not meeting the material specifications, although three months later, the company admitted it had been in error and encouraged us to bid again the next year.

The programs established to help women and minorities secure a fair share of opportunities and actual contracts are, like the general business approach, sometimes successful and sometimes not. There is substantial anecdotal evidence that these programs are not an easy route to business success. What they do offer is an additional marketing avenue for your new company to pursue. You'll need to understand the rules, know how to play the game, and then begin your campaign.

Developing a Set-Aside Strategy

There are four steps involved in developing a successful strategy to utilize "set-aside" programs successfully.

Become Certified by the Proper Authorities

All states have a process by which your company can be officially certified as a Minority Business Enterprise (MBE) or a Women Business Enterprise (WBE). Acquiring this certification will normally make you eligible for the programs of your local government (city or county) and states other than your own. The reverse is usually not true. Acquiring a city or county certificate is no assurance of state acceptance.

You will have to fill out a very detailed form requiring a substantial amount of financial disclosure. The first issue of major concern is where the money to start your venture originated, the object being to substantiate that your company is financially controlled by the woman or minority-group member who is operating it. (When these programs first began, a number of businesses operated by white men started subsidiaries headed by women or minorities; while they provided the appearance of nontraditional ownership, the real economic benefit reverted back to the majority owner.) And so, the first criterion of certification is actual ownership.

The second issue is determining who has operational control. Who makes the actual decisions about every aspect of the day-to-day functions of the business? Is the nontraditional owner knowledgeable enough to make the critical decisions, and is there empirical evidence that he or she is actually exerting that authority? Again, this process is used to disqualify companies that are only fronts and not actually "stand-alone" female/minority enterprises.

After the forms have been completed and reviewed by a committee, an on-site visit is normally scheduled. One or two representatives from the minority business department will come to your office, factory, or job site to see your business in operation and interview you. The purpose of this visit is to make sure that the assets you need to complete the work you say you are qualified for are actually yours and that you are not fronting for another company. Also on their agenda is determining whether you, the stated owner, are actually the hands-on owner. Are you really managing and "controlling" your own business? These are further checks to prevent majority-controlled companies from using minority or female figureheads. The process is time-consuming and may be annoying, but it is a positive factor in assuring that the businesses that need the help are the ones that get it.

Once your company has secured your official state certification, the other local and out-of-state governing bodies may simply issue their certificates. With the exception of one special Small Business Administration (SBA) program, the federal government operates on a self-certification basis. That is, if you say that your business is "owned, operated and controlled" by a woman or minority-group member, that is sufficient to enable you to bid on a contract as an MBE or WBE. However, you are signing the statement in which you certify the status of your company under penalty of perjury. If you are later challenged and have misrepresented the actual status of your company, you could face criminal charges.

The SBA program I referred to as the exception is called the 8A program. Eligibility determination begins with a very intense and time-consuming process for certification as a business run by a "socially and economically disadvantaged person," which is more comprehensive than simply being a member of a minority group. There aren't any formal restrictions against Caucasian women, but few have ever been admitted to the program. Once a company has been accepted, the SBA works on its behalf to secure contracts with a variety of government agencies and sometimes private companies that need minority participation to fulfill contract requirements. The 8A program is a guaranteed fast launch for any new business. The downside is the length of time required to become a part of the program, which can be up to a year. In many instances there is no way of knowing how long it will take: admission is closed periodically because of a shortage of staff at the SBA. This is a complicated way to begin a new venture.

There has been an ongoing controversy within the SBA and in Congress concerning the necessity for this type of program and how long a company should be a part of 8A before it becomes self-sufficient. You will lose most of your guaranteed customers when your participation ends, and if you haven't been developing additional customers, you'll need to start over from ground zero. You might be better off doing this in the first place. As with subcontracting, you can't wholly depend on any one program.

It doesn't hurt to utilize your status as a "special" vendor, but how much you depend on it is your call.

Find the Real Opportunities

Yours is a new company, and you will soon find out that most established businesses in your area have had existing minority vendors in place for some time and are seldom looking for new ones. It's always a good idea to let them know you're here and ready to serve their needs. But your time and energy would be better served by looking at other newer businesses that are developing vendor relationships. Most companies are conscious of the need to develop women- and minority-owned business as part of their supplier base, so if you are the first one to get on their list, there could be good business prospects for you.

Some companies advertise in the paper for suppliers. Prime contractors looking for WBE or MBE participation will place notices in the legal advertising section of the classifieds under the title of bids and proposals. They will list exactly what goods and services they are seeking, and if your business can supply what is needed, contact the company as soon as possible. Many of these advertisers need subcontractors such as your company in order to complete their own contract requirement and may be willing to negotiate a contract with you rather than a competitive bid, which will allow you to maximize your profit potential.

Existing organizations are sometimes pressured by the community into placing special emphasis on development of minority contracting programs. In the past few years, major league baseball has been answering the charges of organizational racism by reaching out to the minority community on many levels. This includes minority vendor programs. Each team is responsible for its own level of participation, but there is committed direction from the commissioner's office in the form of the director of special marketing, Leonard Coleman; a committee of owners who oversees the project; and specific individuals designated in each team's front office. I've met with Al Gordon, one of the two designated contacts of the Pittsburgh Pirates, and attended a meeting of minority entrepreneurs co-chaired by Mark Sauer, president of the team, who is deeply involved in minority business programs in the Pittsburgh area. The Pirates don't make a big public relations deal of their commitment, but spending a few minutes with Al Gordon makes it evident that if yours is a minority business with something to offer, you will be given a fair shake by this sports franchise. Try the team in your town.

Just as the Pirates have a quiet yet committed approach to creating opportunity, some of the most vocal or public supporters may be all talk and no action. For the past few years, I have seen an advertising campaign by a Pittsburgh utility asking women and minority vendors to call on them. Yet many of the company owners who followed up on that request got an indifferent response from the actual buyer. The manager of the program, who also purchased the commodity my company sold, wouldn't give me an appointment. If you don't get a real chance to bid on a company's needs after several calls and visits, go on to the next potential customer. Keep in touch, but don't spend valuable time without getting any return.

Make the Best Approach

The first impression you give any new customer is very important, and it makes no difference whether you are approaching a company as a potential MBE or as a WBE vendor. Whether the company is anxious to have you on board or just wants to give that impression to avoid any appearance of bias, your job is to make a professional approach.

Your first letter or brochure should state the fact of your MBE or WBE status, but the real selling point you want to emphasize is the value of your products or service and how committed your company is to excellent customer service. These are the selling points that you will highlight with any potential new client. Even if a company has contacted you, respond as if it needs to be sold on your capabilities. Never give the impression that you feel that another company must do business with you because you are a "special" vendor.

Even though there are times when your WBE or MBE status will make the acquisition of new business easier than if you were just out competing for it, the result may be only a single purchase, and the purpose may be to get you on the books as a "minority" supplier. Remember that your job doesn't end with that new order, it begins there. You must handle the business and the customer in a professional and efficient manner if you want to become a trusted, regular vendor. The first order from any new customer usually isn't profitable (it costs too much to set up a new account and process paperwork); the real value is in an ongoing business relationship. Your "minority" status is your foot in the door; your performance will determine the rest.

Uncover New Customers Before Your Competition Does

In the twenty years that "set-aside" contracts have been a part of the business landscape, the level of interest, commitment, and enforcement of contract requirements has gone up and down depending on the general political climate and the general economy. Early in the life of these programs, opening up the procurement process in the interest of fairness was felt to be urgent. After some time and a fair amount of negative publicity, there was a backlash against set-aside programs, and they were referred to as "reverse discrimination." In 1989, the United States Supreme Court ruled that many of these regulations were unconstitutional unless they were based on actual proof of prior discrimination. For some corporations, this was the excuse they needed to discontinue purchasing practices that they didn't agree with in the first place. Others were committed enough to track the discrimination and reinstate an affirmative buying policy based on the results of their study. These revived programs are now coming back on stream and are often chronicled in your local paper. One of the biggest, the Port Authority of New York and New Jersey, reaffirmed its commitments in mid-1993 based on its own research. Great chances for business for WBEs and MBEs can be found on the news pages of your local paper. Follow up this information.

Also, many new programs begin as a result of negative publicity about the behavior of an industry or a company. This type of response is partially well intentioned and partially good public relations. Does it matter to you why, or is it just important that a chance now exists where there wasn't one before?

After the Denny's restaurant chain had a number of discrimination charges filed against it, it quickly responded by meeting with representatives of the NAACP to forge an agreement to open up better communications with and develop greater sensitivity to the minority community. New minority purchasing goals were established to direct over $100 million of business to African-American vendors. Any astute entrepreneur should be offering goods and services to Denny's as soon as she sees these sensitive problems beginning to surface. It helps your company, and it helps your customer prove their good intentions.

Read your newspaper and watch the news as if they were sales tools of your new venture, because that's just what they are. What's happening in your community in a general sense has an influence on how you operate your company—use it to your advantage.

Are Set-Asides Needed?

The controversy over the need for and the fairness of special purchasing programs for MBEs and WBEs is not likely to end any time soon. Firms headed by minorities and women continue to be less successful than those headed by their white male counterparts. This can be attributed in part to the newness of the MBE and WBE companies, their lack of access to capital, their limited access to the established business community, and other reasons, including sexism and racism. Set-asides are another way to level the playing field by increasing buyers' awareness of the availability of nontraditional companies. And as long as these attempts are being made, your company should be making the best use of what's available as one phase of your business strategy. But only one. The ultimate goal is to compete and win in an open market. That's a win you can sustain.

9

Location, Location, Location

Finding a Place for Your Business

Carl Umphries began his one-person human resources consulting business from his home to save money. After twenty years in the personnel department of a major midwestern bank, this African-American middle manager found himself reorganized out of a job. Confident that his background as a trainer with special emphasis on managing diversity would be a valuable asset to small and mid-size companies on a consulting basis, Carl didn't even consider looking for a new job. Instead, he put all of his energy into creating his own business. Carl was conservative by nature and without any entrepreneurial experience, and he didn't want to incur overhead expense early in his new venture. He installed a separate phone line in his home, which was answered by voice mail, and he rented a post office box for mail.

The first few months were tougher than Carl had expected, and his confidence was shaken. Feeling that it was time for him to get some advice, Carl approached a friend who had a thriving financial consulting business. One of the recommendations he received was that a box number and voice mail tarnished the professional image he was trying to project to his most desired potential customers. Still unwilling to spend the money for a full-time office, Carl found a secretarial service that would answer his phone, accept his mail, send and receive faxes, and do other "on demand" tasks, and would also provide a conference room for rent if needed. The charge was reasonable, and no long-term commitment was required. Carl immediately signed on and sent out "we're moving because we're growing" notices to his prospects, and his business began to take off.

The new address—and new image—wasn't the only reason Carl's business began to improve, but it was a contributing factor. Your location does say something about your business, and you must determine the right message to send.

There are several factors to consider when locating a new business:

- Are the location, size, and decor of my office critical to my business image?
- Where are my customers located?
- What can I easily afford in my start-up phase?

Location = Image

You do not have to rent a suite of offices in the most expensive office tower in the center of downtown in order to give a professional appearance to your emerging business. As Carl found out, you can use a "shared service" location to create that same impression. In fact, going overboard may give just the opposite message to prospective customers. When I see fancy offices for a new business, I become a bit hesitant to do business there because I know the cost will be passed on to me. In addition, I have consulted with a number of start-up ventures that took on high overhead at the outset and failed because of the burden of those costs.

The business direction of the nineties is to seek the best value in the market. Customers are looking for companies that give the appearance of stability and an understanding of cost control. Finding the right location that telegraphs a "good value" message for your business is a positive first step to success.

The lowest-cost way to begin a business is in a corner of your own home. However, there are trade-offs to working at home. You won't have the cost of rent or travel, and if you have a young family, you may also save the high price of day care. On the other hand, you must consider how many distractions you may have at home. If you have to conduct occasional meetings with clients or business associates, is there a space in your home where you can have those meetings? You will also have to see whether the zoning laws in your area allow business to be conducted from a residence. If you create a lot of traffic, your neighbors may complain and cause you problems.

Location = Customers

A new business must choose a space that is accessible to its customer base. If your customers come to you, make their trip as easy as possible. If yours is a retail business, study the demographics and the traffic patterns in the area you are considering. Investigate the availability of parking and the accessibility of public transportation. Once your business has been around for a while and has developed a following, your customers will be more willing to travel to come to you. In the early phase, make your customer feel valued by locating where you are easy to find and to patronize.

Even if you are serving an industrial market or working as a consultant, you still must consider where your customers are typically located before you set up shop. If you regularly call on them or make deliveries to them, the comings and goings will have a cost associated with them that will have an impact on your prices and profits as well. If the majority of your clients are likely to be in a city location, it may not be wise to set up a suburban office even if you live in the suburbs. If your customers are typically outside of the city—in an industrial area, for example—you can save time and money by locating your business as close to them as possible. It may not have the pizazz of the city center or a fancy office park, but there is a lot of pizazz in banking your profits at the end of each month.

Location = Profits (or Loss)

In most cities, the cost of business property varies widely, depending on the location, size, and condition of the space. Warehouse and manufacturing space can go as low as $2 and as high as $12 per square foot per year in my own city of Pittsburgh. Consider what that means for an annual rental of 5,000 square feet. The low range would carry a monthly cost of $833, and the high range would be $5,000. Quite a difference and quite an impact on your bottom line!

In Pittsburgh, retail space of 2,000 square feet ranges from $6 to $22 per square foot per year—monthly that would be $1,000 to $3,666.

Office space of 800 square feet has a range, also in Pittsburgh, of $4.50 to $28.00 per square foot per year—monthly charges of $300 to $1,866.

After you decide on the image you want to convey and where you want to be in relation to your customers, you're ready to begin your search for the perfect space. Call as many landlords and real estate agents as you can to establish the current price range. Then decide how many square feet you will need and the average square foot cost. Choose a local real estate agent and give him or her your requirements and a certain period of time (a week to a month) to locate a variety of spaces for you to see in person. Calling several agents at one time can create confusion as to which one showed you a particular space first. Remember, agents are paid by the landlord, and it is the landlord's interests that they represent. They want to be fair so that they can make a deal work, but they won't ask for a lower price unless you require them to do so. You are making a decision you will have to live with for a few years, so make it carefully. The choice may very well be the difference between profit and loss.

You should see at least three or four properties in an area before deciding which one would be best for you. Rents are usually based on the prevailing rate for the area, but it sometimes happens that an owner has purchased a building at a good price and set the rental price accordingly. If you don't find an offer you can't refuse, choose the best of the ones you've seen and make the best deal you can.

How to Negotiate With a Landlord

A number of items that are incorporated in a lease can be negotiated between the tenant and the landlord. The three major areas are:

1. The term (length) of the lease
2. The payment structure
3. The leasehold improvements

Term of the Lease

A lease can run from as little as one year to as many years as the parties are willing to make an agreement for. In some rare instances, the term is not in years but in months. These month-to-month leases usually require thirty days' notice by either side for termination. Long leases allow for some stability in your location, and the rent increases are usually kept to a fixed percentage and established at the time of the lease. If you expect your space requirements to remain stable, a long lease may be of value to you. However, if you expect rapid growth, a long lease will prevent you from moving to larger space as you expand.

If you hope for growth but aren't really sure if you'll need extra room, you may be able to put special terms in your lease that will address this contingency—for instance, an option for additional space in the same building or a provision that if your company moves to larger quarters controlled by the same landlord, the old lease will be automatically cancelled and replaced by the new one. Another possibility is a two-year lease with an optional third year.

Most landlords like long-term tenants because there is a cost associated with marketing and renting space. Take as long a term as seems reasonable, but remember that a lease is a legal agreement and your company will be held liable for unpaid rent.

Payment Structure

The second area for negotiation is the rental charge. You would be surprised at how much room there may be in the monetary negotiation. A space that has been vacant for a number of months or even years may be offered with a few months' free rent as an incentive. It doesn't hurt to ask. If you are signing a three- to five-year lease, the building owner may be sufficiently glad to know that a long-term revenue stream is in prospect that he will not mind waiting a few months for it.

Also, consider asking for lower rent in the first year, moving up as the second and third years begin. This allows you to control overhead while your business is in its start-up phase. It doesn't have to cost the landlord anything over the term of the lease. For example, if you are considering office space renting at $400 per month and are willing to sign a three-year deal, the total rental income over the term would be $14,440 ($400 × 36 months). How about making an offer of $250 a month for year one, $400 a month for year two, and $550 a month for year three? As your business gets stronger, you pay more rent and the landlord realizes the same amount, although not having use of the money in year one represents a landlord concession. Many building owners who are willing to work with new business ventures understand the problems, and these landlords would probably work with you.

Leasehold Improvements

The third issue for consideration is known as leasehold improvements. This can include building new walls, installing electrical systems, or doing any additional work your business needs done on the property. In some cases, improvements are the total responsibility of the tenant; in others, owners are willing to negotiate this aspect of your tenancy also. If a building is owned by someone who already has workers on the payroll and access to building materials, the owner is more likely to be accommodating. Ask for everything you want, but be ready to settle for less. The owner may agree to pay for the work when it is and add an additional monthly charge to your rent to repay this.

The best-run entrepreneurial ventures are flexible and have owners who have learned how to be effective negotiators. Here is an important place for you to begin to learn this skill. If you are successful, it will be of direct benefit to your new business.

The Inner City and Enterprise Zones

Many of our inner-city neighborhoods are deteriorating, with both housing stock and business property at risk. You may have grown up in such a neighborhood and be committed to returning. Governments are acutely aware of the problems of the inner cities, and they have responded on a variety of fronts. One is the establishment of community development corporations (CDCs), which were mentioned in Chapters 5 and 6 as a source of training and funds. A CDC also may operate as a nonprofit real estate agency by keeping a database of available business property. Some of the space is for rent by owner, and you won't find it listed anywhere else. When you begin to look in a specific area, check for the CDC and give that office a call—it should be able to send you a printout of its list. Go to the community and look at the property as it could be, not as it may be at present.

Many CDCs have been successful in having large areas of business property designated as enterprise zones. Businesses that decide to locate in these zones benefit from a number of local, state, and even federal programs, including tax abatements, grant (not loan) money to rehabilitate a building for low-income housing or needed retail services, and low-interest loans for the capital to operate these businesses. The red tape can be time-consuming because several layers of approval may be needed, but the cost benefit should make it worthwhile. The number of programs designed to serve as incentives for new business development has been growing, and the federal government has been trying to increase its impact in this effort.

Most CDCs have a loan packager or technical assistance director who can give you much of the information you need.

Consider the business needs of the residents of the community. You may find there is an eager clientele just waiting for
you to open your restaurant, grocery store, or retail outlet.
Many areas have enough local residents to patronize a number
of businesses if only they would locate there. It is certainly
worth your consideration.

You may be starting a small manufacturing firm that has a
number of entry-level positions. A community with high unemployment could provide you with a labor pool and the possibility of state or federal training funds as well.

Of course, there is a downside to locating in an inner-city
neighborhood. Buildings will be older, services may be fewer,
and outside customers may be reluctant to come into the area.
The problem of safety and security is one of main concern. I
wouldn't be naive enough to tell you that crime isn't an issue
to consider, but it should not prevent you from operating a
business where you believe it should be. Taking reasonable security precautions can minimize much of the risk. And the ability to bring jobs and commerce into your own neighborhood is
one of the reasons you want to be in business. I am not preach-
ing from a theoretical viewpoint. For twenty years, my small
manufacturing company operated in a low-income inner-city
neighborhood in Pittsburgh. We operated as good community
citizens, and we were well treated by most of the residents.
Windows occasionally were broken and one car was stolen, but
that was the extent of any real problems. Drugs were becoming
an increasing problem in the area, but the only reason we
moved was the deteriorating condition of the building. I'm now
looking at another inner-city area in which to locate the company. The low cost can ease the monetary burden, and it is
possible to operate a wide variety of businesses from anywhere
the financial incentives are the most favorable.

Business Incubators

Housing a number of start-up businesses in a single building is
a growing method of assisting new ventures from the difficult

days of start-up into growth and ongoing success. The cost of this joint space is normally higher than that of raw space, but a number of shared services are offered, including the use of conference rooms, copy and fax machines, and secretarial services. No doubt this can enhance the professional image you present. However, the real value of a business incubator goes far beyond the administrative. A well-run business incubator includes business counseling and professional services. Part of the admission requirement may be a completed business plan, and the staff or director of the center may even be willing and able to help you develop your plan. Then their job becomes helping you to make your company begin on the right footing.

Be aware that some building owners have added a few amenities, such as a common conference room, and called their space a business incubator. There are no formal requirements for using the name, so don't think that just because a space uses the term, it can provide the services. You should meet a director and not a real estate agent, and interest should be forthcoming in your plans and how you can be assisted to make your venture a success.

In addition to professional help, you will benefit from the friendship and advice of other entrepreneurs. You can learn from one another's mistakes and pass on tips and leads for new customers or even new suppliers. It's an exciting challenge to go into business for yourself, and it can be even more interesting if it is a shared experience.

10

You've Got to Have Friends

Building a Business Network

You are now or very soon will be a member of the business community. Your activity and level of participation in that community are purely voluntary and should be based on your interests, your needs, and the time you can afford to spend in activities outside of your business and personal life.

A good business network is a valuable asset to any entrepreneur as a source of support, information, advice, and leads to new customers and opportunities. It would be a mistake not to join and participate in at least one formal business organization. This gets the name of your company in front of others, which is a form of low-cost advertising as well as a source of business programs that will increase your knowledge and your skills.

Types of Organizations

Your first decision is the type of organization to join.

General Business Groups

Perhaps the best-known business organization is the Chamber of Commerce; every city and town and many smaller neighborhoods have a local chamber. If you are a retailer in an urban business area, you will probably find that most of the major players are very active in the chamber. They will attend a fair portion of the monthly meetings and be responsible for some committee activities, which can include holiday decorations, promotions, and public safety. At times, the members of the chamber will simply join together to take positions about local issues and encourage elected officials to act. Occasionally, the members will contribute money and staff to the sponsorship of an activity. This is more prevalent in smaller communities where the local government has a small tax base and is unable to provide all the resources necessary to promote local business.

There is another "chamber-like" organization—known as a "merchants' " association—that is active in many retail business areas. All of the Chambers of Commerce are affiliated with a national organization, but the merchants' groups are locally organized and controlled. Their main focus is the promotion of the stores in the area through sidewalk sales, joint advertising, holiday business hours—anything that increases sales.

Joining either one of these groups should have a positive impact on your new business venture. There are also a number of groups that are directed to a wider audience—a portion of a whole state or a national constituency. Small Business United, the National Federation of Independent Business, and the National Association of Manufacturers are of this type. In Pittsburgh, we have a local business group that started out as the Small Manufacturer's Council but enlarged its membership base and is now a diverse organization called Pennsylvania Small Business. This group is loosely affiliated with other business groups across the state and a few nationally. Its focus is on legislative issues and member education. Its monthly meetings have excellent speakers, and it sponsors a number of seminars for members. To find such groups, check your local Yellow Pages under "business organizations."

These business groups normally base their membership fee on the number of employees in a company, so if you are a small start-up, the cost won't be excessive. The average would be $200 or so per year. There are benefits offered to all members also, including group life and health insurance. The combined buying power of a large organization makes the premiums so competitive that you may be able to save more on your coverage than you pay in dues.

Another type of general business organization is known as a tip club; the names of a few that are currently operating are Network Professionals and Le Tip International. New ones are forming all the time. Each chapter admits only one member from any profession or trade to avoid competition between members. At each meeting, leads are exchanged as part of the membership requirement. For example, I might know someone who was looking to rent commercial space, and I would give the name to the real estate agent in the group. Or if my company needed a new brochure, I would give the business to the printer in the group. These are good referrals because of the seriousness of the members and the fact that if you don't provide leads to other members, you're out of the group. Meetings are usually held weekly at 7:00 A.M. over breakfast, and the dues average between $75 and $100 per month. Given the commitment of time and money, members of these organizations are not just casual joiners.

Trade Associations

There is a large variety of organizations, some national and some local, directed only at specific professions or industries. These include the local bar association, medical and dental society, hotel association (many have local chapters), and manufacturers' associations. Virtually every industry has a trade association. If there isn't a local chapter listed in your phone book, try calling the Washington, D.C. area for a listing of the national groups, since many are headquartered there.

These groups were formed to influence legislation and trade policy, work on industrywide technical developments, and sponsor joint meetings, trade shows, and conventions for themselves and, often, their suppliers.

As your new venture grows and is able to afford attendance at trade association events, you will find much of what they do of tangible value to you. But you can expect it to cost thousands of dollars, and this may not be money well spent in your early years. Since most trade groups actively recruit new members, it is likely that you can be invited to a meeting as a guest and limit your cost to the travel or event expense. This will allow you to check out the activity of the group.

In addition to judging the effectiveness of the association, you need to decide how you as an individual will fit in and be accepted. In some instances, you may be one of only a handful of women or members of a minority group. This may make no difference, or it may make you feel like an outsider and prevent you from taking full advantage of your membership. A number of years ago, I resigned from the Work Glove Manufacturers Association (our trade group) because anything I suggested was rejected without consideration and I felt completely patronized by the male members. After I forced my appointment to a committee, it scheduled a meeting at a men's club in Akron, Ohio. My feeling was that this was done to discourage me from attending, but that didn't stop me. I even flew in from a trip to Atlanta. Instead of really getting to work, however, the committee made too much fuss over my being in the club. It was a waste of my time and my money.

These groups can be very valuable, and, over time, leadership and attitudes do change. (The Work Glove Association has changed its name to the International Hand Protection Association, and its leadership is more enlightened.) They are a place to share industry information and see trends in their early stages.

Service Organizations

If you are a community activist, you probably started off as a scout, worked your way up through the Jaycees, and are now a Rotarian, Lion, or Kiwanis member. As a youth, you joined for activity, then for social reasons, and now you are motivated by a sense of community service. While it is important to remember your responsibility as a good citizen, there is a direct benefit to your business life. You will work with and get to know other members of your business community on a very personal level. You will learn about their companies, and they will learn about yours. This is good for public relations and good for sales. These are friendships that may last a lifetime and that often continue after individuals move on and move up. They enlarge your business "network" as well as your personal relationships.

I first met my banker as a member of the Pittsburgh Jaycees, and in that environment, we developed not only friendship but mutual respect as we worked on projects together. He saw me as a competent businesswoman, and over the years, when I have needed help and advice from a banker, I have been able to call on him for assistance. The service groups are where many such relationships form and grown.

You can also learn new skills as you work on a wide range of activities. If you're not sure of your selling ability, try to move ten books of raffle tickets and you'll get better at it as you go along. If you've started a one-person shop and have concerns about how you'll manage other employees as you grow, agree to chair a project and you will be required to manage other members towards the ultimate goal. The four years I was an active member of a Jaycee group was as valuable to me as an advanced business degree, and I did work that was of some value to my community as well. Such efforts are rewarding, but they are also time-consuming, and I have seen people neglect their own businesses in favor of organization work. That is a risk a start-up entrepreneur cannot afford.

Gender- or Race-Based Organizations

There are a growing number of groups whose members are all women professionals and business owners or all black or Hispanic professionals and business owners. Many of these groups were formed because women and minority-group members were not permitted or welcomed as members of other associations. I remember how relaxed and relieved I was to join a group of businesswomen and not feel as if I were on display or under scrutiny, as I had in groups where I was one of a few women. I could finally discuss many of my business problems, particularly those that concerned the sexism I had to deal with on a regular basis. We could all laugh at our common annoyances—at the number of times we were called "honey" on the phone, ignored at a meeting, or publicly demeaned by someone who harbored his own prejudices. The anger dissolved in laughter. The support we gave one another was critical to our growth in business.

And we learned general business skills together—aspects of the law, insurance coverage, investments, estate planning, and sophisticated marketing skills. When the environment is relaxed, the learning is easier.

There is a wide array of organizations to consider, from the National Association of Women Business Owners to the National Association of Minority Automobile Dealers and the Women Construction Owners and Executives. A selected list is included in the Resource Guide at the end of the book. Some associations have one large national chapter and hold an annual convention, other national organizations hold regional meetings on a quarterly basis, and a number of these groups have local chapters that meet monthly. Dues are usually set accordingly—from as low as $60 annually to several hundred dollars and the cost of the meal or travel and hotel.

These groups meet to socialize, to educate (themselves and the public), to further legislative action beneficial to their industry, and to serve as role models for others wishing to follow in their footsteps. Among all these goals and activities, you will find one of interest to you.

If at all possible, you should join at least one group of your specific peers. You owe it to yourself. I have yet to meet anyone who didn't derive some benefit from these organizations. You also owe it to your peers to support their efforts. Forming these nonprofit groups is an enormous undertaking, and keeping them running is a daunting task. Whatever public knowledge or public pressure is brought to bear by a professional organization, you will benefit from it. And you owe it to those who follow to show that there is strength in the solidarity of the groups that will someday address their challenges.

Your Need for Business Groups

Starting out, your main concern is and should be the business you are trying to develop. Your hours may be very long and your work never-ending, but you are making a mistake if you isolate yourself within the walls of your business. You need the socializing, the relaxation, and the information available through business groups. Your company needs the exposure. You will benefit from personal friendships with other business owners.

Don't join everything at once and then have no time to participate. Find out what is available, attend a few sample meetings, and start out slowly. Belonging to a few different groups can become one of the most valuable aspects of your business life.

11

We Are Family

Hiring and Motivating Good Employees

Many small businesses start out with a single employee, the founder. And then the day comes when there is too much work for one person. On that day you become something you probably aren't prepared to be—The Boss! It seems to many of us that it is much easier to be the employer than the employee, but you are about to learn that each role brings its own set of challenges.

The experience of working in a small business is far different from that of working in even a mid-size company. It is more personal and far more intense. Even the size of your space is smaller, and you will spend more time in the actual presence of your employees. This requires a style of leadership different from the typical corporate model—more casual and more flexible.

If you have the extra work now but think that you're not yet ready for the responsibility of hiring and managing others, try using subcontractors (secretarial service, data processing service, etc.) until you have more time in business under your belt. But the day will eventually come when you will hire your "first" employee.

Finding Good Employees

The most expensive way to find workers is through a commercial employment agency because its fee may be 10 or 12 percent of the first year's wages. Few people looking for work can afford to pay the fee, and your new business may not be in a position to even assist with an advance. It is unlikely that your job opening would be given any attention.

Less expensive but often very time-consuming is advertising in the newspaper. Depending on the job offered and current economic conditions in your community, you could receive over a hundred replies. Then you begin the process of review, scheduling interviews, checking references, and finally making a decision. This process can keep you very busy for several weeks—keeping you from running the business.

Your state employment office will be glad to post your opening for free, but you will have to list your company address and phone number. As a result, you won't be able to control the number of phone calls or visits without appointments, and this could become quite a distraction. It can also take time to have your name removed from the agency database after the position has been filled.

One of the best ways to find new employees is through personal referrals. Let your family, friends, and other business associates know that you are looking for some help and ask if they have anyone to recommend. In the current job climate, there are many people, from entry-level to experienced, looking for employment, and you should be able to locate someone with the potential to help your business grow.

Another source of candidates is community-based social service agencies, such as church-sponsored self-help groups for the unemployed. Many YWCAs and YMCAs offer training and employment counseling and would be happy to refer their clients. Some of the social service agencies dealing with older adults (over fifty) also do job development and may be able to match a mature worker with your job opening. The services of these agencies go far beyond just taking information; they work individually with their clients to identify skills and help in job searches. Therefore, the counselor should be able to give you more information about your candidate to aid in your interview.

Educational institutions, from high schools to trade schools to colleges and universities, are also a good place to find workers, both part-time and full-time. Many students need some work to supplement their income while attending school, and many high school counselors assist by contacting local employers. Trade schools and colleges are usually willing to post available part-time jobs in student service offices.

Most schools have placement offices to help their graduates find employment. If you are looking for an entry-level college or trade school graduate, let the appropriate officer at your local school know and he or she will be happy to work with you. The benefit of a recent graduate is state-of-the-art skills; the drawback is lack of work experience.

Interviewing a Potential Employee

Now that you have your list of candidates, it's time to schedule a meeting in person. Make sure to get a resumé or a completed job application before the interview so that you can review it and perhaps check some references. If any questions arise from the check, you can get clarification in person. Even if your applicant has been fired from a previous job, this doesn't mean that he was totally to blame. Keep an open mind and trust your own instincts.

If you have conducted only a few of these interviews and are still a bit uncomfortable, rather than covering it up, you may want to be candid about your feelings. It will be obvious that yours is a new company, so your own inexperience won't be a surprise.

Start off by describing what expectations you have for your company, and allow your candidate to ask questions. Here is where you'll begin to get a sense of whether she understands the business and how you expect to run it and make it grow. In a small start-up, the first employees are a real factor in the success or failure of the venture. If you can find someone to share your dream, you have made a major step forward.

Check out all the skills you require for the job. If equipment is used in the work, let the candidate try it out so that you can observe his level of expertise. If you are going to hire someone to learn on the job, make sure she has the aptitude for the work.

A strong word of warning when hiring general office staff: If the job includes keeping your books (and it often does), make sure that you find someone with basic business knowledge; you may want to arrange a meeting with your accountant before the starting date. Many new companies get into serious trouble because of poor accounting, inaccurate information about their costs and level of profits, and, worst of all, tax forms which are filed incorrectly, late, or not at all. This can threaten the very future of the business, and the best way to prevent it from happening is to make sure the person responsible for filings understands how to do them *and* their importance.

Checking References

Before making your final selection, be sure to do a complete check on references. You may think you have good instincts about others, but it is best to be cautious. Here's what happened to someone who wasn't.

Debby operates a successful travel agency with one key employee. Her problem has always been finding a good third person. The "leftover work" is boring follow-up tasks, and the pay is fairly low. During one hiring marathon, a young man appeared at the office, full of enthusiasm and great promises about new business he could develop. In the rush of activity, no reference check on past employment was made. JR was hired on face value, and he lasted less than a month. Before it was over, he had cashed a bad check, borrowed other money, and reportedly told several clients that he was buying the agency. In short, he created a good bit of chaos. When outsiders started calling JR and demanding repayment of the money they had loaned him, he took off without a trace. The experience was time-consuming and energy-draining, and it could have been prevented. After he was gone, Debby started calling names he had given her to see if she could locate him and get restitution. What she found was a pattern that would have warned her from the beginning had she checked.

Paying Your Employees

New companies have tight budgets, so your salary offers to new employees will be fairly limited. When considering a wage range, remember that there are more costs involved than the money paid directly to the employee. You will have the employer's contribution to FICA, and state and federal unemployment taxes as well. These will be at least 15 percent of wages. Your workers' compensation insurance must be added, as well as any benefits such as life or health insurance. We are fast approaching the time of mandated health insurance, so consider that fact. Bottom line: Each $100 of wages may have an additional $40 of cost attached. The minimum wage with benefits and taxes attached is closer to $6.00 an hour actual cost than to $4.35.

Wages for experienced managers or professionals can be fairly competitive, although they have become more flexible since the massive numbers of corporate layoffs have occurred. You cannot expect a high performer with a choice of other positions to choose your company if your pay structure is far below the prevailing scale, but if you can come up with an adequate starting wage and your candidate sees the potential for growth and success in your new venture, you may be able to attract a truly high-level employee. Don't be intimidated out of at least offering a job to someone who seems to be out of your league. Many refugees from large corporations are attracted to the excitement of small business. You won't know unless you ask.

Perhaps in the early stage, you can make up in flexibility and future promise what you can't pay in current wages. Having a schedule that allows for child care, school studies, or other interests may be worth something to a potential employee. It may require extra effort from you, but it could be worthwhile. You may also offer raises tied to the growth and performance of the company. Not only does this ease your financial burden in the early stages, it gives your new employee a tangible incentive to contribute to the overall success of the business—a win for both of you. Now is the time to be creative—isn't that one of the reasons you became an entrepreneur? A warning here: Promises made to an employee about future compensation could be construed as a verbal contract and enforceable in court. Don't offer anything you don't expect to be able to provide.

Becoming an Employer

The first person to be trained is the boss: on how to be a good employer. And the first lesson is to think a job through in advance. Many new entrepreneurs bring on employees because their own workload has expanded too much, but they haven't determined how to divide the job between themselves and their workers.

The corporate response to this would be to write a job description, but few entrepreneurs have the time or inclination to do so. If you are one of the unique ones who are so inclined, by all means go ahead. If you're not, then at least come to a verbal agreement with your new employee about the scope of his tasks and ask him to write up a brief memo that you can both go over and clarify. You'll save a lot of conflict down the road.

On a regular (daily or weekly) basis, you will want to meet with your employees and review work to be accomplished, where the responsibility rests, and when tasks are to be complete. Create a memo or a short form to recap the work assignments. Since your business will grow and change, you and your first employees will be training each other in the early days. But a key issue is clarity of understanding. You can expect an employee to complete work only when she clearly understands that it is hers to do and knows fully how you expect it to be done. Be fair.

Motivating Employees

We all like to be proud of the result of our work, and our commitment is made stronger by the amount of our own ability that has contributed to that work. This is the theory behind worker empowerment, which is being utilized at large and mid-size companies. In essence, this is about giving workers the tools and the authority to do their own job without constant supervision. This allows them to take personal pride in the result.

This method of motivation is absolutely logical, yet it is difficult for many new entrepreneurs. When it is your money and your career on the line, it isn't easy to allow others to have control of even a piece of the decision making in your business. You may be told that you need to delegate responsibility, but you may be unsure of how to do so comfortably.

Consider this aspect of your work when you are first hiring new employees. The lowest-cost individual with little experience may not inspire in you the level of trust you need if you are to delegate real authority. It may be worth it to your future success to spend more in the beginning and hire someone that you feel comfortable about putting in charge of a project.

Another technique to releasing authority is to be open and honest about how difficult it is for you. Once you discuss it, you'll begin to see how unwarranted most of your concerns really are. You and your employee may be able to codevelop a reporting system that allows you to know exactly how things are progressing without looking over someone else's shoulder.

None of us likes being treated like a child. Empowerment is about treating one another as adults involved in work of mutual interest and responsibility. You can let go if you try.

You can also motivate others with a reward system. It may be a cash bonus, a gift of nominal value, a special luncheon, or merely extra time off. It is a way of singling out the accomplishments of another and saying thanks. Everyone wants to hear those sentiments, and most people will work harder when they know they are appreciated.

Handling a Difficult Employee

You may have been careful about hiring, you may have done a good job at training, and you may even be a good motivator, and yet you may still find yourself with an underperforming worker. Perhaps you were misled at the outset, or there may be a personal issue in someone's life that distracts from his work. But anything that affects the performance of your company must be dealt with as soon as it becomes evident.

You'll want to start with a face-to-face meeting to spell out the problems and make sure that both of you understand what was expected and what deficiencies have occurred. Determine what needs to be done to correct the problem and a time period (ten days, two weeks) in which the improvement is to be made. You want to be fair, but remember that a single poor employee in a small-business setting can destroy the entire venture. After the meeting, summarize the agreement in writing and give a copy to your employee. You are creating documentation that you may need later, and you are also allowing one additional chance to clarify any lack of mutual understanding.

If time passes without any improvement, you must take the unpleasant action of termination. I have done it in person, over the phone, and in writing, and there is no easy way to fire someone. Make it as short and direct as you can—state the reason clearly. Get the individual off the premises as soon as possible so that the level of disruption will be kept down. If pay is owed and you can give the person a check immediately, do so. Otherwise state exactly when the check will be mailed. Give specifics in writing as to the termination of any other benefits.

If you must handle this through the mail (usually because of attendance problems), do so by certified mail with a return receipt requested. Enclose any pay that is owed and other information required. Keep a copy of your letter.

Working together with good employees to build a business

is a satisfying experience, and you don't want to allow a single nonperformer to demoralize the group. Action is uncomfortable but necessary.

Ensuring Diversity in Your Work Force

Once you become a business owner and begin to build a team to create your vision, you may well learn about one of the benign causes of prejudice. We are all more comfortable with people who are similar to us in background and outlook. A business owned by a woman and employing only women will find its dynamics changed by the inclusion of a single man. A group of African-Americans will find themselves less comfortable when a nonblack comes on board. This is one of the reasons that organizations begun by white males fought so hard to remain white male institutions. But being comfortable is not the best way to build a vibrant company, and most of us believe that diversity is an issue of fairness as well as good business sense. People of both genders and all races have something of value to contribute, and each and every business should welcome a variety of perspectives. After all, your customers are diverse; shouldn't your work force be as well?

There are equal employment laws that cover hiring in companies with over twenty-five employees, and other regulations oversee businesses with government contracts. You cannot deny a job to someone because of gender or race. However, white males are not a "protected" class, and you could theoretically refuse to hire any and not find yourself in legal difficulty. But you don't want to systematically deny anyone an opportunity, particularly if you have been a victim of systematic discrimination. Be honest with yourself about how you expect to build your work force by finding qualified employees. Make a conscious effort to be fair.

On the other hand, with your special sensitivity, you can give opportunity to others of your gender or with your own ethnic or racial background that the traditional business owner cannot give, and this well may be part of your mission. You may understand the problems of inner-city youth or working mothers and be able to structure a job that allows time for extra training or split shifts to accommodate school hours. You can serve as a role model or "special friend" to young people who need to see future possibilities for themselves and will find them in your success. This is a very worthwhile goal. If you have any doubts about your policies, contact an attorney.

There are many satisfactions in creating a business, some monetary, some beyond money. Having the chance to create a positive influence in someone else's life and watching her or him grow as a result is a worthwhile effort and a part of your payback.

12

The Customer Is Always Right (and What to Do If He's Wrong)

Attracting and Keeping Customers

You have found some capital, a location, a set of advisers, and perhaps employees, and you're ready to go. Now you will begin to really deal with the focus of your business—the customer! But attracting customers is only phase one. Serving them well, keeping their business, and using their recommendation to create more customers is one of the key elements of success.

Think about why you frequent a restaurant, gas station, grocery store, or any type of business, and incorporate all the positive experiences into your own company. Always give your customers more than they expect and let them know how important they are to your business. It seems so simple, and yet we all have experienced the annoyance of waiting on hold on a phone line, not being waited on, or being treated just plain rudely. Such experiences make us wonder if other business owners have thought about it. Perhaps they have, but they haven't figured out how to put it into practice.

Make sure that your employees understand how you expect them to deal with your current and prospective customers, and set an example by your own behavior. Make it clear that when the choice is between serving the needs of your customers and doing the work that you have assigned to them, your vote is with the customer every time. If a client has taken up a large block of time, you might pitch in and help finish the other tasks that need to be done. This sends a strong message about priorities.

If you have gone into a store and not been waited on because the sales help was busy filling out forms or straightening up stock, you can remember feeling that if your business was not important to the company, you would take it elsewhere. That's exactly how your customers will feel about your new venture unless you go out of your way to ensure that their interests are really the driving force behind your company. This is the focus that you should establish on day one and continue throughout what will hopefully be the long life of your business.

Discovering and Keeping Your Key Customers

This may be a strange concept to someone with a new business, but you can't sell to everyone, and you really don't want to try. Your business will be better at some things than at others. Trying to be all things to all people creates a company that does a lot but excels at very little. Be careful not to let the demands of a few keep you from serving others who will be important to your success.

Linda Moore started a restaurant serving great Caribbean food that was based on her old family recipes. Part of the personality of this type of cooking is in the spices. During her very first week in business, an older couple came in for lunch and returned a few days later for dinner. They seemed happy to find a place so close to home but were rather unsure about the food. Linda enjoyed visiting with them when it was quiet and was happy to cook special requests with less spice to conform to their dietary requirements. As the restaurant caught on and became busier, this extra work became a burden, and other customers had to wait to be served while Linda took time to prepare the couple's unseasoned version. Then other people began asking for "off menu" items, and things began to get out of control.

Finally, Linda realized that she had to use her time and energy to serve the largest number of customers, and that did not include the older couple, even though she had become fond of them. But a happy compromise was reached—every Wednesday evening, the menu would include a "special" unspiced dish made primarily for her new friends but available to other customers along with the items they normally expected. The couple was flattered enough to make their regular visit on that evening, and other customers who loved the high spice began bringing along less adventurous diners for the midweek special.

Sometimes you have to find a way to completely stop serving a single demanding client in favor of the rest of your customer base. It is never easy to turn down business, particularly when you are new and each dollar of revenue seems very important. If it comes to this point, be sure that you are gracious and attempt to find the individual or company help somewhere else. You may want to solicit the business at a later time, and you want to leave a good impression.

Making Sure Your Customers Know What You Need

Just as it is important that you be on the same wavelength as your employees, you need to be on the same wavelength as your customers. Part of your job is to educate them in how your company operates most efficiently and how your efficiency will best serve their needs. If you need two weeks to make delivery, let your customer know that in advance. Don't make promises you can't keep just to get the order. You won't perform, and you'll lose the business in the end.

Credit granting is another thorny issue for a new business. Few start-ups have sufficient working capital to grant long-term credit to their customers. In many businesses, it is customary to give terms of net thirty days, and if your money is out longer than that period of time, you may experience difficulties. If you aren't being paid, ask for payment in a polite way. Explain your situation and see if you can't find a sympathetic ear. In the end, a customer who won't pay you isn't worth having.

Handling Customer Complaints

Sometimes things go wrong. It may be your fault, or it may be beyond your control. A product you resell may have come in with a defect, repair work may have been incorrectly completed, or you may have misquoted a job and be forced to charge a higher fee. No one is perfect, and you and your employees will make mistakes. And sometimes customers complain without any reason at all.

The first key in dealing with a customer's dissatisfaction is to listen patiently to the entire story before making any decisions as to what you must do. In the first place, you are showing that you are concerned about what has happened, and that means a lot to people in our stressful environment. Also, you may hear something that will give you a clue to exactly what went wrong with the product or the transaction.

Keep calm if at all possible, and suggest several alternatives as solutions. Perhaps a full return is in order, and you will take it up with the manufacturer. The answer may be a partial refund because of a minor defect or a credit against the next order as a show of goodwill. Try to find a meeting ground that will not cost you more than you can afford but that still seems a fair solution to the problem at hand. You are probably on a financial tightrope, and it wouldn't hurt to gently make that point to your client.

Why bother to jump through these hoops at all? First, because you really should be about the business of quality and customer satisfaction—it's the way to develop a long-term successful company. And second, you should understand that a growing number of unhappy customers will prevent the growth and success of any commercial concern. Word gets out—far fewer people will spread the word about the virtues of a business than will be willing to share their complaints. There will be times when you won't be able to negotiate an acceptable solution, but you should always give it a try.

What to Do When a Customer Becomes Rude or Worse

People say things when they are angry or under stress that they wouldn't normally say, although what they say may be an indication of what they believe. This may take the form of rude or foul language—patronizing sarcasm or out-and-out racial, ethnic, or sexual slurs. Some of us overreact to these references because we have heard them too often over the years. After over twenty years in business, when I hear a particular tone of voice and the words, "listen, honey" on the other end of the line, my blood pressure starts to rise. But I try to keep myself under control.

You need your customers, and you want to serve them well. But that does not include taking abuse. It demeans you, and it demeans all of us. If there is a valid complaint, try to deal with it. If it's just meant to be rude, don't bother. Give the offender one calm chance to reconsider his behavior and then end the conversation. Be firm and be brief. Gently hang up the phone, walk out of the offender's office, or ask the person to leave yours. Don't think you can engage in dialogue that will change someone's mind or behavior. It's not possible and it's not worth it.

It is disconcerting to lose a customer whose bias prevents him or her from recognizing what you have produced or accomplished. This reality can shake your confidence in being able to create a truly successful business. If you are a woman in a traditionally male business, you will be a novelty to some customers and an annoyance to others. Spend your time and energy on those who are willing to develop a good professional relationship with you, and don't worry about the others.

A minority company serving a nonminority market will also face some undeserved resistance, but this does not have to be a roadblock. There is a world of potential customers—find the ones who are open to your new business and serve them well.

The key is to respect yourself and believe that you are deserving of the respect of others. Give no less and expect no less.

Earning a Good Reputation and Getting the Word Out

Any start-up venture needs to establish its credibility. This is done one customer at a time, and there are no good shortcuts. Start out with the attitude that you are going to treat everyone fairly, and then go one step further. Give your customers more than they expect—in your time, in service, and in satisfaction. Be aware of their needs and responsive to their concerns. Treat them the way you want to be treated, and your company will grow.

Here's one place where delivering a needed enterprise to the minority community works in your favor. If you take the risk of starting a venture that meets a need when others aren't willing to take that risk, many customers will be in your corner at the start and remain loyal throughout. People appreciate a business that goes the extra mile. Many locally owned stores and services have a following that could never be duplicated by a chain or an absent owner.

New customers who are pleased with the product or service that you provide can be a great source of referral business. Don't wait for them to tell their friends and associates; ask them to do so. Run a promotion with a discount for the second shopper or diner or client. Give a discount to the one making the referral. Conduct a contest asking for leads; with each one provided, a chance in a raffle will be awarded. The prize may be tickets to an event or a gift certificate for your own store. The point is competition and appreciation. The more people you have interested in your success, the more successful you're likely to be.

Converting doubters into believers is a real challenge, and getting people to patronize your business on a regular basis takes effort. Make their satisfaction your goal and you're on your way.

13

Today Is the First Day

Getting Ready to Open

It may have been a long time since you first decided that you wanted to be in business for yourself. I'll bet you thought the day would never come when you would see your plans become a reality. Well, that day is almost here, and now you should go back one more time to make sure that you've covered all the bases.

Here's a checklist of items to review before the doors swing open:

- [ ] Have all tax identification numbers and tax licenses (e.g., sales tax) been issued?
- [ ] Has your accountant set up your books so that you can begin recording all income and expense transactions?
- [ ] Has your attorney reviewed all leases and agreements that your venture requires?
- [ ] Have you opened a business bank account? (*Do not* combine business and personal funds.)
- [ ] Have you introduced yourself to the bank manager and told him or her about your business?
- [ ] If you are renting space, have all the proper inspections been made, and do you have an occupancy permit?
- [ ] Have you located all the suppliers you will need to start and found backups for those that may be critical?

- [ ] Have you hired the workers you will need and carefully checked their backgrounds and references?
- [ ] Have you established payroll procedures and a special payroll account?
- [ ] Have you made sure your employees understand the goals of your company, and do they know that the customer comes first?

Along with preparing to receive and serve your new clients, you should also be working on ways to attract them. Your marketing efforts should begin early, escalate just before opening, and continue as long as you are in business. Here's a good plan of action.

Before the Company Opens

1. As soon as your business plan is complete, use it as a tool for informing individuals who may be customers or may be able to refer customers. A lot of work was involved in creating the plan—put it to use.

2. Have business cards printed as soon as you have an address and a phone. Even if you haven't nailed down a location, you can rent a post office box. Hand the cards out wherever you can, and if you have an answering system on your phone, use it to announce information about the actual start-up of your venture.

3. Join clubs and organizations as a way to meet new people and let them know about the "soon to be opened" venture. Hand out your cards at meetings along with any other promotional material you may develop.

4. Create a mailing list of family, friends, old classmates, and former business associates so that when you open, you can send them a formal announcement.

Around the Actual Opening

5. Send out information to your mailing list and invite special guests to a "preview" opening.

6. Attend meetings and pass out the "official" notice to group members.

7. Meet with other business owners in your area and invite them to patronize your new business. Use theirs whenever possible.

8. If yours is a retail business, start off with a Grand Opening Sale and promote it as much as possible in your market area. Try using teenagers to pass out fliers in the neighborhood and put them in doors.

9. Offer a free service along with what you sell. For example, a new antique store may have an appraiser in for the opening days to offer free evaluations.

10. Send a press release detailing the unique feature of your business to the local papers and periodicals. If you are the *first* woman to open an automotive repair shop or the *first* African-American to start his own investment firm, that may be newsworthy enough to get you a mention in the regular news section of the paper. Don't neglect the local TV stations either; they have human interest slots to fill, and your business may be just what they're looking for.

11. Offer special discounts to members of a club or organization that might be a source of potential business. If you open a restaurant and there is a large building, business, hospital, or college nearby, pass out 10 percent off certificates good for your first few weeks in business. You won't lose money, and you should attract a following.

12. Create a direct mail campaign and purchase a mailing list. This can be expensive (hopefully, you accounted for it in your plan), but a well-created brochure sent to the right individuals can have a big impact.

13. Hire a celebrity to attend your grand opening. A local radio personality of just-below-superstar athlete may be enough to attract a crowd.

14. Barter your goods or services to the local media for advertising. Radio stations often are willing to give air time in return for credit in restaurants, travel agencies, and printing companies. If you have anything to offer, give it a try.

A good radio blitz just before a new business opens can be just the push the business needs to take it over the top. Don't ignore television because you think it is too expensive. With so many cable stations, you can target just the right viewer for far less than you think. The cost to consider is production costs—an effective ad should be staged on video, and that can cost several thousand dollars.

On the Big Day

15. Make the business come alive—open with a bang, not a whimper. Decorate your office or your shop and fill it with people who are proud of your accomplishment and will make you feel successful from day one.

16. Throw a party and make everyone feel special, welcome, and wanted back.

In the First Few Months

17. Maintain your enthusiasm for your work and your new customers every day that you are open. Be there to let people know that you are involved and are not just collecting the receipts.

18. After the first series of promotions, come back with a second and a third. There will be a drop-off after people come to "check you out." Encourage them to come back by making it worth their while. A contest . . . a fashion show . . . a special demonstration—keep the business alive.

19. If possible, develop an ongoing mailing list of customers so that all promotions and special deals can be offered to them in a special mailing. Everyone likes to be an insider.

20. Talk to your customers and listen to what they have to say. Your customers have information, ideas, and criticism that will let you know how you're doing and what you could do to improve. Asking for their suggestions involves them and cements their loyalty—especially when you put their suggestions into action.

I've given you twenty ideas for finding and keeping the customers you will need to take your venture over the top. I wouldn't be surprised if you could think of twenty more, and they all would have merit. Anything you do to energize your company, the people who work there, and those who patronize it is worthwhile. The major mistake to avoid is not doing anything. You have worked hard and worried a lot in the weeks and months leading up to your "first day," but now is not the time to slack off. This is the birth of a new company—one which you hope will grow and prosper. But the only part you have completed is the labor. Now you must nurture your creation into independence.

Congratulations—you must be proud!

Resource Guide

Agencies That Provide Information

Loans and Assistance

Small Business Administration
1441 L Street
Washington, DC 20416
SBA Answer Desk (800) 827-5722

This line has a series of prerecorded messages that give information about starting a business, getting financing, exporting, and general business assistance. The line operates electronically, but you can also be connected to a business counselor on request.
Other SBA phone numbers:

(202) 606-4000 Main line
extension 222 Minority Business Enterprise
extension 258 Women Business Enterprise

Federal Government Agencies—Small and Disadvantaged Business Utilization
Each of these offices (there is one for virtually every agency) monitors opportunities available to small, minority-owned, and women-owned business in that particular agency and its prime contractors. Some agencies also have separate minority business offices. The phone numbers for SDBU liaisons for each department follow:

Department of Agriculture
(202) 447-7177

Department of Commerce
   (202) 482-1472
   (202) 482-1936 Minority Business Representative

Department of Defense (see various services)
   Army (703) 697-8113
   Navy (703) 602-2700
   Air Force (703) 697-9249
   Defense Logistic Agency (703) 274-6471
   Defense Commissary (804) 734-3263
   Defense Intelligence (202) 373-2822
   Defense Nuclear (703) 325-5021
   Defense Fuel Supply (202) 274-7428
   Advanced Research (703) 696-2379

Department of Energy
   (202) 586-1596 Office of Minority Economic Impact

   This agency provides loans and bid assistance to MBEs
pursuing Department of Energy contracts.

Department of Health and Human Services
   (202) 690-7300

Department of Housing and Urban Development
   (202) 755-1428

Department of the Interior
   (202) 208-3493

Department of Labor
   (202) 523-9148

Department of State
   (703) 875-6823

Department of Transportation
   Federal Highway Administration (202) 366-0693

Department of Treasury
   (202) 566-9616

National Aeronautics and Space Administration
   (202) 453-2088

General Services Administration
   (202) 566-1021

U.S. Postal Service
(202) 252-1730

Veterans Affairs
(202) 233-7611

National Science Foundation
(202) 357-7875

Environmental Protection Agency
(703) 305-7777

Other federal agencies that can be of assistance:

Government Printing Office (a wide array of business publications is available)
(202) 783-3238
Register of Copyrights
(202) 707-3000
U.S. Patent and Trademark Office
(703) 308-4357
International Trade Administration
(202) 482-2060
Trade Information Center
(800) 872-8723

Associations and Organizations

General Business

American Management Association
135 West 50th Street
New York, NY 10020
(212) 903-7915

Offers a wide-ranging program of seminars, many of which are applicable to the needs of small and mid-size companies.

American Marketing Association
250 S. Wacker Drive
Chicago, IL 60606
(312) 648-0536

Has more than 100 local chapters.

Center for Entrepreneurial Management, Inc.
180 Varick Street
New York, NY 10014
(212) 633-0060

Conducts many courses and seminars.

National Association of Home-Based Businesses
10451 Mill Run Circle
Suite 400
Owings Mills, MD 21117
(410) 363-3698

Provides a quarterly publication as well as seminars and expos.

National Association of Small Business Investment Companies
1199 N. Fairfax Street, Suite 200
Alexandria, VA 22314
(703) 683-1601

"Venture Capital—Where to Find It" lists 160 small investment companies nationwide and is available for $10.

National Business Incubation Association
One President Street
Athens, OH 45701
(614) 593-4331

Offers a directory of available incubators.

National Federation of Independent Business
600 Maryland Avenue SW
Suite 700
Washington, DC 20024
(202) 544-9000

Small business lobbying groups.

National Restaurant Association
1200 17th Street NW
Washington, DC 20036
(202) 331-2429

Offers publications and information on how to start a restaurant.

Small Business United
1155 15th Street, Suite 710
Washington, DC 20065
(202) 293-8830

Congressional lobbying group.

For Women Business Owners

American Women's Economic Development Corporation
60 East 42nd Street
New York, NY 10165
(800) 222-AWED

Training, assistance, and counseling for women business owners.

American Business Women's Association
9100 Ward Parkway
Kansas City, MO 64114
(816) 361-6621

National Association of Black Women Entrepreneurs
P.O. Box 1373
Detroit, MI 48231
(313) 559-9255

National Association of Women in Construction
327 S. Adam Street
Fort Worth, TX 76104
(817) 877-5551

National Association of Women Business Owners
600 South Federal Street
Suite 400
Chicago, IL 60605
(312) 922-0465

Women Construction Owners and Executives
P.O. Box 883034
San Francisco, CA 94188
(415) 467-2140

For Minority Business Owners

Minority Supplier Development Council
15 West 39th Street
9th Floor
New York, NY 10018
(212) 944-2430

Has 50 chapters throughout the United States that act as liaison between minority companies and corporations wishing to do business with them. Sponsors trade shows and seminars.

National Association of Minority Automobile Dealers
16000 W. Nine Mile Road, Suite 603
Southfield, MI 48075
(313) 557-2500

National Association of Minority Contractors
806 15th Street NW
Suite 240
Washington, DC 20005
(212) 347-8259

National Association of Black-Owned Broadcasters
1730 M Street NW, Suite 412
Washington, DC 20036
(202) 463-8970

National Association of Black Accountants
220 I Street NE, Suite 150
Washington, DC 20002
(202) 546-6222

National Black MBA Association, Inc.
180 North Michigan Avenue
Suite 1515
Chicago, IL 60601
(312) 236-2622

National Conference of Black Lawyers
2 West 125th Street, 2nd Floor
New York, NY 10027
(212) 864-4000

National Society of Black Engineers
1454 Duke Street
Alexandria, VA 22314
(703) 549-2207

U.S. Hispanic Chamber of Commerce
4324 Georgia Avenue NW
Washington, DC 20011

Periodicals

Minorities and Women in Business
P.O. Drawer 210
Burlington, NC 27216-0210
(919) 227-5601
(919) 222-7455 fax

Subscription rate $12.00/year (6 issues)

Black Enterprise
Earl S. Graves Publishing Company, Inc.
130 Fifth Avenue
New York, NY 10011
(212) 242-8000

Subscription rate $19.95/year (12 issues)

Minority Business Journal
P.O. Box 3543
Pittsburgh, PA 15230
(412) 682-4386

Subscription rate $8.50/year (6 issues)

Small Business Reports
P.O. Box 53140
Boulder, CO 80322
(800) 234-1094

Annual subscription $98.00 (12 issues)

This monthly publication is packed with practical, hands-on advice on how to run an efficient and profitable business. It has regular features on management, legal issues, and sales strategies as well as a book digest in each issue.

Books

Growing a Business, by Paul Hawken (Fireside Books, 1988).

This book is a classic—an extraordinary view into what it means to the individual to start and grow a business. It gives information along with insight.

Succeeding in Small Business, by Jane Applegate (Plume, May 1992).

This book answers 101 questions that most entrepreneurs will face at one time or another.

Guerrilla Marketing, by Jay Conrad Levinson (Houghton Mifflin, 1984).

Another "classic" business book, the first of a series of "guerrilla" books by Levinson including one on finance and a second one on marketing. Excellent advice for small start-ups.

Growing Your Home-Based Business, by Kim T. Gordon (Prentice Hall, 1992).

Sustaining Knock Your Socks Off Service, by Ron Zemke and Thomas Connellan (AMACOM, 1993).

Free Help From Uncle Sam to Start Your Own Business, by William Alarid and Gustav Berle (Puma Publishing Company, 1992).

SBA Hotline Answer Book, by Gustav Berle (John Wiley, 1992).

The New Venture Handbook, Second Edition, by Ronald E. Merrill and Henry D. Sedgwick (AMACOM, 1993).

How to Become Successfully Self-Employed, by Brian R. Smith (Bob Adams, Inc., 1993).

Index